Residential Child Care and its Alternatives:
International Perspectives

For my friend Andrew.
with compliments

Friedhelm

Helsinki, FICE-Congress 2008

Residential Child Care and its Alternatives:
International Perspectives

Edited by Friedhelm Peters

Published by Trentham Books in partnership with FICE –
Fédération Internationale des Communautés Educatives

Trentham Books
Stoke on Trent, UK and Sterling, USA

Trentham Books Limited
Westview House   22883 Quicksilver Drive
734 London Road   Sterling
Oakhill   VA 20166-2012
Stoke on Trent   USA
Staffordshire
England ST4 5NP

First published 2008

British Library Cataloguing-in-Publication Data
A catalogue record for this book is available from the British
Library

ISBN: 978 1 85856 409 8

Designed and typeset by Trentham Print Design Ltd, Chester and
printed in Great Britain by Hobbs the Printers Ltd, Hampshire.

Contents

Foreword

The Fédération Internationale des Communautés Educatives (FICE) was founded in 1948 to provide support for people working with children and young people in the aftermath of the Second World War, with the aim of establishing high standards of service. Publishing has therefore been one of its key activities over the six decades since it was founded, and FICE has a long list of publications to its name, including books, journals and reports. They have been published either by FICE-International, the umbrella body, or by the professional organisations which act as FICE's National Sections in each country.

FICE-International is now pleased to be working with Trentham Books to initiate a new series of books covering different aspects of work with children and young people. Since a substantial proportion of FICE's members work with children and young people who have to live away from their birth families, residential care and its alternatives are the focus of this, the first book in the series. It is an important area of work, and one which suffers from misinformation and prejudice, and it is hoped therefore that the ideas in this book generate debate.

I would like to thank Friedhelm Peters for editing this volume, the authors for their contributions, the FICE-Inter Editorial Board for their advice and support, the FICE Federal Council for backing the proposal, Robert Shaw for his meticulous work on the texts and proofs and Trentham Books for their encouragement.

David C. Lane
Chair, FICE-Inter Editorial Board
Vice President, FICE-International

Acknowledgements

This book would have not been published without the assistance of many people. Therefore I want to thank all who supported this publication in one or another way. I want to thank the FICE Board and especially the members of the FICE-Editorial Board: Malay Dewanji (India), Emmanuel Grupper (Israel), Sören Hegstrup (Denmark), Andrew Hosie (Scotland), Martti Kemppainen (Finland), David Lane (England), Karin Lauermann (Austria), Monika Niederle (Austria),and Helga Stefanov (Austria), who gave me the opportunity to edit this book and assisted with ideas in obtaining contributors.

Special thanks to David Lane, who negotiated with the publisher and brushed up some foreign English and to Monika Frank from the Erfurt University for Applied Sciences, who did a wonderful translation job for two chapters of this book. Special thanks also to all contributors to this book, for their work and their patience with me and for holding to the strictly given guidelines for the articles.

Last but not least I want to thank my friend Josef Koch and my wife Sigrid for their profound spiritual support when the going got rough, and also to Sigrid for the time I spent with the book instead with her.

Friedhelm Peters

List of Contributors

James P. Anglin, Ph.D., Professor for Child and Youth Care at the University of Victoria, Victoria, Canada, and Associate Vice-President Academic Director of International Affairs. Email: avpadia@uvic.ca

Roger Bullock, Fellow, Centre for Social Policy, Warren House Group at Dartington, Devon. Email: rbullock@dartington.org.uk

Bojan Dekleva, Dr., Dipl. Sociologist, Professor at the University of Ljubljana, Faculty of Education, Co-editor of *Socialna Pedagogika*, the Slovenian journal for social pedagogy. Email: bojan.dekleva@guest.arnes.si

Emmanuel Grupper Dr., Head of the Socio-pedagogical Department at the Beit Berl University College and Director of the Residential Education Department at the Israeli Ministry of Education, President of the Israeli Residential Education and Care Association (FICE-Israel)

Peter Hansbauer, Dr. phil., Dipl. Social Pedagogue, Professor at the University of Applied Sciences, Muenster. Email: hansbauer@fh-muenster.de

Kaija Klap, Social Worker, Family Therapist and Supervisor at Lauste Family Therapy Centre, Family Therapy Trainer at the Centre for Further Professional Education at the Summer University, Turku.

Alenka Kobolt, Dr., Dipl. Psychologist, Professor at the University of Ljubljana, Faculty of Education, Co-editor of *Socialna pedagogika*, the Slovenian journal for social pedagogy Email: alenka.kobolt@guest.arnes.si

Irit Mero-Jaffe, doctoral student at Ben-Gurion University of the Negev in Beer Sheva, Israel, educational and social studies evaluator for various institutions, an evaluator and research fellow for the Research and Evaluation Unit at Beit-Berl University College, teacher at the School of Education at Beit-Berl University College.

Marc Noom, Ph.D. Assistant Professor in Developmental Psychopathology at Leiden University, Faculty of Social Sciences, Department of Special Education, member of the board of the Dutch section of FICE. Email: noom@fsw.leidenuniv.nl

Friedhelm Peters (Editor), Dr. phil., Dipl. Sociologist, social worker, Professor at the Erfurt University of Applied Sciences, member of the editorial staff of the journal *Forum Erziehungshilfen*, Co-editor of the series *Basitexte Erziehungshilfen* (Juventa-Verlag, Weinheim). Email: peters@fh-erfurt.de

Wolfgang Trede, Dipl. Pedagogue, for many years Secretary of the German FICE-Section, since 2003 Head of the Child and Youth Department Böblingen (Kreisjugendamt Böblingen), Co-editor of the series *Basistexte Erziehungshilfen* (Juventa Verlag, Weinheim). Email: mayer.trede@t-online.de

Keith White, PhD, Director of Mill Grove, a residential community in London UK, Associate Lecturer at Spurgeon's College, University of Wales, former Chair of the National Council of Voluntary Child Care Organisations, former President of the Social Care Association, and Chair of the Operations Team of www.childrenwebmag.com Email: Millgrove@btinternet.com

Micha de Winter, Professor of Social Education at the Department of Child and Adolescent Studies at the Utrecht University, Netherlands, trained as a developmental psychologist, and as a family therapist; main topics, both in teaching and research are social education, prevention of childhood and youth problems and social participation of young people in neighbourhoods, schools and residential care.

Mechthild Wolff, Dr. Phil., Dipl. Pedagogue, since 2002 Professor for Pedagogy at the University of Applied Sciences Landshut, Dean of the Faculty of Social Work, member of the editorial staff of the journal *Forum Erziehungshilfen*.
Email: mwolff@fh-landshut.de

1

Introduction:
Residential child care and its alternatives –
professional approaches in a discursive field

Friedhelm Peters

1: The Discursive Order of the Field of Child and Youth Care

Residential care has for various reasons been under discussion for a long time. One reason is that the placement and education of children and adolescents in residential care homes is, unless only a short-term measure, certainly one of the most powerful forms of youth welfare affecting young people's life stories. Another is that it bundles together 'assistance', 'protection' and 'control' in a special way. A third is that residential care is questioned, 'because [residential homes] are costly, ineffective and, in too many instances, abusive' (Beker and Schwartz, 1994, p276). Or they show poor performance in relation to outcomes such as education, vocational training and job participation, thus raising the matter of effectiveness. Or, as Alan Johnson, Secretary of State for Education and Skills, says in his Foreword,

> This Green Paper shows that for many of the 60,000 children [in England and Wales] who are in care at any one time, childhood and adolescence are often characterised by insecurity, ill health and lack of fulfilment. This is terribly sad. And we can hardly be surprised that it results in many children in care underachieving educationally and getting nowhere near fulfilling their potential as adults. (Department for Education and Skills, 2006, p3)

Other authors consider the situation described as being true, but insist that there will nonetheless be 'a group of older troubled children or adolescents for whom good residential group care options can be appropriate' (Beker and Schwartz, 1994, p283). But there is agreement that residential child care has to improve. The discussion among professionals, researchers and practitioners – and sometimes the public and politicians – is about the directions in which to go. Such discussions represent not only ways of speaking about something, but function as discourses (Foucault, 1979b,a) which constitute a specific field both as symbolic order and as material practice.

As in any discourses, their actual meaning and effects are primarily governed by their expression in a contemporary social practice, which is already structured, motivated and contextualised – in modern societies usually through some kind of professional or other, mostly science-based, discourse. Their general function is to signify, define and regulate, not to explain. Therefore their message is more or less prescriptive. Their typical consequence is not an account of a social conflict, but rather the distinguishing of what is 'right' or 'wrong' in a given practice. In this dimension they work as 'social censures' (Sumner, 1990). As 'materially rooted in the dominant social relations of the epoch, such ... [discourses] must soon take on a more generalised character as other people internalise them ... They tend to be the ones that are institutionalised in the discourses of the state' and the public, the media etc. They are 'only ever formed in practical conflict with opposing groups and therefore are always subject to continual resentment, resistance and redefinition by these oppositions' (Sumner, 1990, p27) and therefore we observe changes over time.

The concepts of juvenile welfare and of juvenile and societal protection, for example, as well as the nature of the education which inmates in the institutions could expect, are highlighted by the traditional names for the institutions: 'house of rescue' (Wichern, 1964) or 'compulsory education institutions'. Although this explicit naming, which was applied to the earlier, non-pedagogically based institutions, had has its day, the idea of reform and the concept of education as legitimate compulsion have in no way disappeared.

2: The situation in the reform years: the 1970s and 1980s

Before the late 1960s and 1970s you could conceptualise children's institutions, especially residential child care, as part of the 'youth in trouble system', including porous boundaries between the child welfare, juvenile justice and mental health systems, all based on the concept that it is deemed necessary to separate children and youth from their environment and provide them with appropriate educational, vocational, and treatment services under controlled circumstances. At the end of this child and youth management process you would have found (and sometimes find even now) secure institutions or the children being passed to another segment of the 'youth in trouble system'.

This was, and is, not random – it is an outcome of how the whole system is organised. You can find these outcomes anywhere such a specialised system had been institutionalised (Millham *et al*, 1978).

> The reading of several hundred voluminous files on secure unit children is a sobering experience. They are an indictment of the child care system. Children are shuffled from one short term placement to another in the vague hope that they will stick somewhere. Some boys have had eight placements in a year ... They return occasionally to assessment centres for additional uncomplimentary labels and then they are on their way again. (Kahan, 1994, p105)

This was seen not only as an ongoing process of labelling children to make sure that the child or youth in mind would pass the criteria for the next programme or institution, not only as the permanent use of symbolic violence by threatening the child or young person that they could be transferred to another, maybe even more severe or more highly structured, institution, if they would not conform, but also as a system of organised non-responsibility, which needed to be changed or even closed. The main arguments arose from the applications of results of a critical sociological understanding of people-processing organisations, especially of the sociology of deviance.

The 'labelling-approach' (Rubington and Weinberg, 1968) and especially Goffman's analysis of the 'total institution' (1968) showed pedagogues, academics and practitioners in the field of child and youth care work how organisational impacts worked on clients' histories. This was most clearly shown in treatment institutions in which 'harsh identity-stripping and mortification processes and all-enveloping organisational routine resocialise the individual to his new inmate role' (Schur, 1973, p130). From an organisational standpoint the problem of an individual crisis or personal need of assistance seemed to be to some extent a problem of management or organisational routines. Thus, the focus of the critical organisational analyses broadened the insights of the problems of institutional (residential) care to the bureaucratisation of help and to children and their needs coming under the regulation of hierarchy, impersonality, specialisation and systematic formal rules. The residential home turned into a people-processing or socialising system with from time to time and place to place greatly varied coordination, organisational specificity and rule consistency, in which individuals are passed from one stage or unit to another with selection processes occurring and cases dropping out at each stage.

During the 1970s and 1980s, partly provoked by the student movement of the late sixties and some neo-Marxist and feminist thought, too, but generally more influenced through the above mentioned adoption of the 'interpretative paradigm', for example by the theories of 'symbolic interactionism' and through 'critical theory' (Habermas, 1990) and its manifestation in critical social pedagogy, a reform process started, which, with hindsight, led to a major modernisation of the whole field (Hansbauer, 2008; Trede, 2008).

'Everyday life' was a concern. The term implies a lack of reference to those who focus on institutions as relatively enduring structures and have a preference for the fluid and the mobile.

These thoughts emphasised the means of interaction or relationship without neglecting the meanings of social structures. Following these theories, all social meaning is constituted, secured and renewed only through social interaction, as also are education and organisations (Mollenhauer, 1972). Organisations as well as professional authority are seen to be based on the ability to create and apply a set of cultural-cognitive and normative constructions that provide guidance in numerous types of uncertainty – built up in a defined field of and by diverse actors, both individual and collective. Such an institutional view includes the conceptual models that guide the roles available to individual actors and the forms applied to collective actors, the logic that governs behaviour in the field, and the governance structures that exercise control over field activities, ie cultural-cognitive, normative and regulative constructions.

But in applying these more general theories within an administrative setting (youth administration) and/or in residential child and youth care work, you have to pragmatise their inherent rationality and their implicit practical approach. Therefore 'normalisation' acquired a wide range of meanings in education, housing or dealing with problems; decentralisation and empowerment as well as prevention and regionalisation or a social area approach and higher involvement of, and assistance for, families etc became key concepts. Even if these categories in a strict sense might be pre-theoretical, they are meaningful concepts or theoretical frameworks, which might offer a new generative social practice. They supply the practices (and practitioners) with their objectives and knowledge and forms of reflexivity.

For residential child care this meant speaking about de-specialisation, responsibility and reliability, continuity and relationship, about residential child care becoming a suitable place for living instead being a treatment system, about flexible responses to the needs of children and young persons without consideration as to whether they were staying in a facility at the time. Normalisation means a radical change in the philosophy and practice of residential child care. All in all this was a reasonable shift to an everyday-life based approach (*Lebensweltorientierung*), even if there is no simple one-to-one relationship between complex ideas or rationality to the change of given structures of a field of practice. When we take a closer look at real developments, we always find some kind of mixture of different ways of thinking and styles of reasoning, or in other words of 'discourses and counter-discourses'.

As an example you can identify a more psychological or even psychiatric based model of special treatment. Better performance and outcomes were sought from residential child care through sophisticated diagnoses and assessment procedures, the use of some kind of, mostly behavioural, therapy, behaviour modification programmes, in which re-inforcers such as points, marks, and privileges were used to promote desired behaviour, or of a therapeutic milieu in small-scale facilities or groups, sometimes with reference to the theories of Bettelheim (1950, 1974) and Redl (1966) or the attachment theory of Bowlby (1953).

In practice both approaches, although discursively distinct in different professional fields or academic disciplines, might not have been as sharply distinguished as it might appear here, especially as both paths together led to a new quality of child and youth care work and a differentiation of the supply spectrum of residential as well as non-residential services and, at least on the continent, a process of professionalisation of the staff and the field as a whole. For example, the general qualification of 95 per cent of the staff working in the field of child and youth care and also in residential child care rose to degree level or three years plus in the most developed countries such as Denmark, Germany or the Netherlands.

To summarise, we can say that the process of modernisation which took place in most European countries (although there are still many differences due to different welfare regimes and strong national traditions and cultures (see Hamberger *et al*, 2006) in the dimensions of legislation, professionalisation and differentiation can justifiably be seen as amounting to an impressive professional story of success on the part of the social pedagogical services and residential child care.

The profits of an always expanding and differentiating structure of child and youth care work are strong professional routines, professional expertise, individualised services, and its combination of humanist values and top-down interventions, as well as a supposed close matching of problems or needs of the clients to specialised organisations. At the same time there are losses too, because the more specialised any system is, the more selective it will be. The modernisation of the child and youth care sector followed the fundamental logic of the modernisation of modern societies which increase their efficiency through differentiation and a general culture of specialism. This leads to the unintended consequences of differentiation and a highly selective structure. The existing phenomena of exclusion and poor services for children and their families thus have not been reduced but, on the contrary, have even been to some extent aggravated.

3: The discourses of the 1990s: playing the market game and the new role of professionals

After the late 80s we were confronted with new discourses, new demands and questions, especially arising from neo-liberal ideas and new forms of governance such as the 'new public management' and, in parallel, the 'market/management discourse'.

Neo-liberalism was adopted by many western governments to legitimate the attack on the bureaucratic welfare state and its inherent professionalism (White, 2003). 'Neoliberalism promotes an agenda that is characterised by competition, privatisation, and the reform of public institutions, using managerial ideologies that emphasise the four 'Ds' – decentralisation, devolution, deregulation, and delegation – and codifying policy and accountability' (Besley, 2006, p184). Other authors name the same processes as the 'triple E' initiatives of economy, efficiency and effectiveness or lodge these activities more generally in the wider range of 'new public management' (Otto and Schnurr, 2000). The underlying philosophy is, more or less, taken from the political and economic theories of F. von Hayeck (1944) and the Chicago School of Economics (Friedman, 1962) and enriched with elements of the rational choice theory and a human capital approach. They emphasise 'methodological individualism' and the notion of the '*homo economicus*' based on assumptions of individuality, rationality, and self-interest.

Perhaps most importantly for the child and youth care system, policies influenced by neo-liberalism involve the dismantling of the welfare state through commercialisation, the contracting-out of services, targeted services and the promotion of notions of self-responsibility. Under the political doctrine of neo-liberalism there is nothing or little distinctive or special about education or children's services; rather, they are services, products or commodities to be treated like any other to be traded in the marketplace (Peters, 1999, 2001).

As the principles of markets or quasi-markets are applied to the social services and the child and youth care sector, it is interesting that the effect is frequently the opposite of the rhetoric. Part of the appeal of markets is their perspective 'from below', arguing for greater power to the grassroots in the form of consumer choice. The process of contracting out services, however, has often been to increase the power and control of government and local state authorities. NGOs or not for profit agencies that were previously supported with an operating grant or refinanced for the services delivered are now required to tender for specific services that the government purchases. No longer is the agency free to develop its services in the way it thinks best, to establish innovative programmes or to provide an alternative to the government which used to be the chief justifications for non-governmental welfare in general.

Under the current system of contracting, the control of government, central or local, is much stronger; the agency must meet the government's agenda or it will not receive funds or get clients. In this case, it is actually the managerial discourse of centralised, top-down control that is operating – introducing new forms of dependency as well as accountability under the apparent aim of making services more efficient and targeted. Within the managerial discourse this requires more accurate measurement of inputs and outcomes, and more stringent monitoring of front-line worker activities. This, in turn, implies more things to be measured, counted, timed or recorded by staff, and thus an increased administrative load (for England and Wales see Petrie *et al*, 2003).

Furthermore, where there is an increase in upward accountability of workers to management, it is most likely to be accompanied by decreased accountability downward to the client or outward to the community. In the managerial approach, accountability is usually defined in terms of reporting to management, with appropriate statistics about the service delivery representing the positivist obsession with measuring and counting everything, even processes that do not lend themselves to being readily measured or counted (Peters, 2006b).

This is where another line of thought becomes apparent: quality or quality discourses, the emphasising of evaluation or evaluation research, and evidence-based-knowledge. To wield the power that derives from the introduction of quasi-markets into functional systems such as child and youth care, the administration has to show that all this is being done with the intention of solving complex problems. With respect to its financial and societal responsibilities, the administration buys only good services and therefore needs evidence. Therefore, the production of knowledge or evidence has the double function of producing legitimacy for the political system and knowledge-based solutions at the same time.

> If the measures are made and interpreted within an economic rationale (by combining efficacy with efficiency or even replacing efficacy by efficiency on the level of measurement), and if the flow of resources depends on the decisions made ... on the basis of this measurement, then the effect of the generated evidence is disciplinisation because ... a new rationality of regulation is formed. (Sommerfeld, 2005, p16)

All these principles not only restructure the organisation of services and the inherent knowledge base of child and youth care, but also affect the direct interactive processes between worker and clients. The technocratic utilitarian rationality of evidence-based practice with its emphasis on applied knowledge (the so-called 'Mode 2 knowledge' Fisher, 2005, pp130ff) that is empirically based through randomised controlled trials as the gold standard of evaluation (for a more sophisticated version of evidence-based practice, see Shaw, 2005, pp82ff), and even more specifically the 'what works' movement, tend to reshape both professional and organisational identities on the basis of suggesting that modernisation will be achieved through auditing, priority and target setting, monitoring, inspection and evaluation, or, in other words, through evidence-based performance management or practice.

According to a common and widely accepted understanding, evidence-based practice is 'the conscientious, explicit, and judicious use of current best evidence in making decisions about the care of individual clients' (Sackett *et al*, 1996). The aim of scientific activity in this field is to give decision-making a solid basis by offering practitioners a body of systematically compiled and organised knowledge statements, sometimes prepared and delivered by state or private central bodies such as the Swedish Institute for Evidence-based Social Work, the English Social Care Institute for Excellence (SCIE), the Center for Evidence-based Social Services (www.cebbs.org), the Campbell Corporation and a lot of others (Fisher, 2005 or www.dfes.uk and the links you may find there) to enable them to find, select and use the interventions that are most effective and appropriate, in other words, interventions that work.

Thus Cullen and Gendreau can state that 'the challenge that lies ahead is to use science to develop evidence-based [measures] that not only tell us what not to do but also what to do' (2001, p334), for example:

- focus directly on risk behaviours and problematic attitudes and target factors that have contributed to the problem

- deploy structured approaches with clear SMART (specific, measurable, achievable, relevant, time-limited) objectives and adopt methods that have structure and require active involvement in problem-solving

- match degree of intervention to risk

- deploy strictly directive approaches and styles and use cognitive, behavioural or, at best, cognitive-behavioural methods whenever possible that focus directly on changing thinking and behavioural patterns

- above all, strictly ensure that the completed work fulfils declared aims and methods through programme integrity, that is, avoid drift, objective reversals or non-compliance (Davies, 2000; Ziegler, 2005).

Being sceptical about the evidence-based practice/what works movement is not to doubt a necessity for professionals to be 'scientifically informed'. Neither is it to deny the obviously convincing insight that social work's interference in human life conduct cannot be legitimated by the mere fact of the consumption of welfare services but by the effects and the practical values this interference actually has (Kaufmann, 1976). Yet we should keep in mind that this insight is hardly an offspring of the relatively new 'what works' movement.

> The ideal of a research minded and reflective practitioner with a broad knowledge base has always been a central part of the description of 'the good professional' in terms of the 'professional approach' in social work [and social pedagogy]. The 'professional approach' in social work (Dewe and Otto, 2002), however, differs significantly from an arising 'what works' movement suggesting that statutory practice guidelines are to be designed which are based on randomised control trials pretending to deliver an uncontested truth about what professionals are to do and what they are not to do. Thus the 'what works' approach may even present a vision of an antipode to professional judgements by requiring social professionals to serve within the guidelines and policy laid down by authorities, subject to instructions gleaned from research and managerial orders (Ziegler, 2005, p34).

Professionalism in social work and social pedagogy is closely related to the claim that social work and social pedagogy, as professions in the field of welfare production, have the relatively autonomous competence to make decisions on the basis of their professional knowledge and capability and with reference to their own categories and ways of quality control and disciplinary reflexivity (Dewe *et al*, 1992, 1993; Sommerfeld *et al*, 2005, pp201ff).

There are still some reasons to doubt the functioning of evidence-based knowledge in practice in fields like social work in general or especially in child and youth care, which are due to the inherent interaction structure of these person-orientated services or pedagogical actions.

1. We have to take into account that any mastering of most crises depends on the collaboration of the client. Professional performance therefore is only one aspect of this co-operative process and the outcome depends highly on the quality of the co-production between professional and client. This is not to suggest that some special form of treatment is being prescribed, but it is necessary to develop an individual manner of problem-solving to enable the specific clients to play their co-productive parts and to meet their subjective definitions of the situation or crisis. And this is why, for example, negotiations about an intervention plan are so important and different from most kinds of assessments.

2. There is the question whether in fields of practice which are structured through individualised cases and individualised approaches, knowledge which is produced in experimental or quasi-experimental research designs, is useful or not. The answer tends to be 'not', because 'with this design it is presupposed that both the framing conditions as well as the processes leading to the outcome would be constant, so that comparisons would be possible between different sites where a program is applied. This reduction of complexity is not admissible when we take into account what we described above as the structure of professional action' (Sommerfeld *et al*, 2005, p203).

The evaluation of programmes, if at a high level of data aggregation, as is done in randomised controlled trials or other kinds of experimental designs, offers little benefits for workers in the field of children's services.

> Even if we leave aside the fundamental scepticism about the epistemological and methodological premises of these approaches, and if even all programs of social work would have been studied, the evidence produced only supplies information that a program on selected indicators has a comparably high or low success rate ... This certainly is of some interest, but ... as long as this type of knowledge is not related to the specific conditions of ... an [individual] arrangement of resources and processes, then the professional cannot learn [much] from this kind of evidence (Sommerfeld *et al*, 2005, p203).

An evidence-based understanding of risk factors and related programmes might be useful for political decisions on policy strategies that try to influence or compensate for the living conditions under which children grow up (poverty, poor housing conditions, schooling, the system or organisation of child and youth care, ecological conditions etc), because such strategies have to and can only start by influencing or changing these more distant risk mechanisms, which interfere in individual lives more indirectly by using the media of law, money or organisation, while concrete services for children or families work with interaction and therefore always start, if ever, by trying to work on 'near' concrete and individualised risk factors and are always based on co-production between worker and client(s) – the core of the structure of professional action.

But there is another aspect. As professional actions are basically social actions, they are generally contingent even if structured; no interaction can be reproduced in exactly the same way, which results from the very nature of the social structuring of every day life. Besides this, we have to take into account that any kind of child and youth work is organised in some way or another. From a sociological system theory point of view, such organisations function as systems, which, described very briefly, constitute themselves through separation from their natural or social environments and operate by their own rules or autonomously (*autopoietisch*), respectively in a modus of self-reference. Persons are seen not to be members but to constitute the 'environment' to systems as well as 'psychological systems'. As all systems operate autonomously (*autopoietisch*), persons, too, operate like all systems. This leads to a phenomenon that Luhmann and Schorr (1982) called the 'structural deficit of a technology of education;' that briefly means that there is no reliable causality between any intervention and result on behalf of the autonomous (*autopoietischen*) character of persons. Or in other words, what works in one case with one class with one problem does not necessarily work with another. There is a gap that only can be closed by professionals.

It seems to us that it is no chance that the implementation of the new public management and its emerging managerial-market model, as roughly outlined above has not yet fully entered the European practice of child and youth care work, as a small expert review in fourteen European countries has shown (Peters, 2006a). Indeed, it has already been cut back in some countries which were the first to introduce it, such as the Australian state of Victoria (Peters, 2004). Only in England and Wales, Finland and the Netherlands has this model, with distinctive features, been introduced into practice under very different circumstances and with outcomes which differ hugely.

While in Finland and the Netherlands these approaches are based within a highly developed professional culture, mostly driven by target agreements and contracts, organised within a strong local or regional setting, and with spaced responsibilities and spaced working principles and self-evaluation, the opposite seems to be true in England and Wales. It is not only that the professional social-pedagogical culture is missing as a basis of child and youth care work. The attempts to improve child care work and especially residential child care are, among other things, more centralised (even when services should be provided at community level), more group- or problem-targeted, more specialised, monitored by central or state agencies or inspectorates, implemented top-down and mostly evidence-based (www.dfes.uk).

It is no surprise to academically trained social pedagogues, whose education combines broad scientific knowledge, research (Thiersch and Rauschenbach, 1984), practical skills and a more general competence to work as well in kindergartens, day care, recreation centres, streetwork, in-home services for children and families as well as with older people and who are trained to use or manage a group or a milieu too, that the outcomes of a more or less strictly evidence-based approach are poorer than those which are more social-pedagogically based (for a comparison of England, Denmark and Germany see Petrie *et al*, 2003) because evidenced-based practice generally underestimates the problem that the correlation between scientific knowledge and theory and professional action is by no means trivial.

The idea of a linear and instrumental transfer of knowledge from science to practice and of transformation into interventions is too simple and does not take into account the findings which have come out of research on the use of knowledge. From this research we know that de-contextualised knowledge and also empirical data are often transformed on the long journey from theory into practice, to an extent that they are sometimes completely distorted when they arrive in a practice context. Practitioners are critical thinkers (the idea of the 'reflective practitioner', Schön, 1987) and the more experience they have, the more they will question things instead of automatically accepting everything.

It has to be accepted, therefore, that the transfer of knowledge is more complex than has been assumed. It seems more appropriate to think of knowledge transfer on the part of the person addressed as an activity in which different forms of knowledge are not only built in or adapted or selected but actually integrated: they are brought into relation to each other. Knowledge is developed and transformed into a hybrid form by placing different bodies of knowledge into a meaningful relationship to each other. The result is new knowledge. In the case of professionals, the crucial knowledge base of practice is exactly such a form of hybrid knowledge, in which scientific evidence has been brought into a meaningful relationship with a body of tacit knowledge, general methods of interventions and their personal experiences.

Practitioners generally have to contextualise all kind of knowledge to the conditions of their distinctive practice, and there are different knowledge horizons, too, which have impacts on their performance, as for example results from other social sciences, organisational beliefs, ethical principles and values, questions of gender, every day experience etc (Beck and Bonß, 1989; Dewe *et al*, 1992), while evidence-based practice is conceptualised as a simple procedure of selection of programmes and decisions. Although this problem has been partly recognised (Gira *et al*, 2004; Walter *et al*, 2004), it has not brought about a correction of the underlying transfer model. 'In the vision of the representatives of evidence-based practice, the scientists have always been in the role of the senders of messages, whereas the practitioners, practice managers and organisations have been the ones to receive and implement the messages' (Gredig, 2005, p180).

4: The aims of this book

The arguments outlined above, as well as the above mentioned research (Peters, 2006a), show very clearly that in countries with a strong professionalised and theory-based social pedagogical tradition structuring the field of child and youth care, there is still an ongoing process of discussion favouring a professional approach in children's services, even if there is some sense of pressure to improve the quality of work, to increase accountability and improve documentation as well as consciousness about costs, and attempts to cope with the new demands which arise from the ongoing process of modernisation. There is a general speeding of social processes, rationalisation and growing scientific knowledge, especially the challenges of evidence-based knowledge production, from political decisions (the reorganisation of welfare regimes, the implementation of the NPM etc) and other societal developments such as globalisation, poverty, social exclusion etc.

Clearly, not all of these questions can be answered in this book, but it offers insights gathered from an ongoing discussion about child and youth welfare, and especially child and youth care and residential work under changing conditions. It emphasises an international perspective, not in the manner of a comparative study but through learning from differences and similarities. It shows how social pedagogues analyse their practice and what solutions they do offer. And as this book emerged from the FICE context, it also provides some insight in the lively discussions within FICE.

We are arguing not only for an improvement of residential child care but also for an up to date understanding of critical professionalism. The contributors set out to show how and under which circumstances residential child care or its alternatives might be an up to date response to the needs of children and youth. In short, in emphasising a critical professional role, most of them are arguing for changes in, and a defence of, residential child care, as well as for structural changes in the child and youth care system as a whole and thus for a changed understanding of residential child care.

Such a critical professional habit ('*habitus*', Bourdieu, 1994) consists of partly contradictory presuppositions, such as respect for the autonomy of clients' lives and experiences and the priority for every-day-life evidence, strong orientations towards social biography and living conditions at the same time, scientific knowledge and professional apprenticeship, reflected identity, hermeneutic competencies etc. And last, but not least, there has to be responsibility and the will to act more participatorily. The latter includes, among other things, accepting the service users' views and their judgements about being helped as the most important elements of evaluation. Both approaches will offer new resources. Hereby practitioners will be guided by a scientific discipline of social pedagogy, which takes the route from practice to theory back to practice (Kobolt and Dekleva, 2008).

The alternatives to residential child care are mostly to be seen as inherent, if they are accompanied by a shift of the underlying philosophy of care in the direction of the home being a suitable place of living, and by structural changes as well as a strong professionalism, which is grounded in a self-reflective (scientific) social pedagogic discipline (Dewe and Otto, 2002).

5: The contributions

In accordance with a discipline and practice which claims to be self-reflective, studies not only refer to social pedagogical practice and to the circumstances of its clients and their capabilities to cope with their every day life; they also examine organisations as well as the social functions of child and youth care and what are seen as social problems and the organisational mediated professional reactions or interventions to these problems too (Hornstein, 1998). All these practices are related to special, field-related discourses of the child and youth care system within changing welfare governance regimes, including specific, international or cross-cultural differentiated traditions of dealing with problems of children and youth and their families.

Using such a perspective, Wolfgang Trede outlines in his article how the process of modernisation has already changed residential child care and gives some hints why its different appearances and uses in European countries differ in relation to different cultural traditions. But he also shows that there are some similarities in the direction of the development of child and youth care related law, the age of the children and, above all, in the direction of 'making children strong', not at least through greater participation. Participation thus seems to be one factor of a secure base, an experience Keith White describes in his contribution with respect to the attachment theory of John Bowlby and the Mill Grove experiment. Going back to the history of child and youth care and the relating legislation primarily in England and Wales, Roger Bullock discusses the contributions of the UK to child and youth care policy, practice and research. He highlights the historical and special features (among other things, the unique influences of elite residential schooling) of the English child and youth care, which, till the reforms of the 1960s, was seen as the leading professionalised approach in Europe. This practice, however, is today increasingly determined by regulation in the public sector, with different impacts, as there is, for example, at least in comparison with many continental countries, more research since the 1980s, and more interest in the question of disseminating empirical knowledge.

Peter Hansbauer's central thesis is that the sociopolitical changes which started in the 1960s initiated developments which undermined the legitimacy of traditional patterns of practice in youth services and thus prepared the ground for an accelerated diversification of youth services in the 1980s and 1990s. Using Giddens' 'theory of structuration' he analyses the development of German residential child care since the 1970s and the altered patterns of interpretation and rules of appropriateness which emerged within youth services.

The next contribution can be read as a continuation of the previous topic, but aimed at future developments and arising from different points of view, representing different parts of the discourses in the field of child and youth care. James Anglin seeks to engage the issue of systemic change in child and family services and concludes radically that the root of our traditional helping services, and their frequent failure, is a fundamental misunderstanding of what it means to be human, and therefore policy makers, practitioners and researchers must shift their thinking from partial and therefore dehumanising responses to people's situations. He shows a holistic way ahead and clarifies some implications for practice, policy and research.

Part Two of the book starts with Alenka Kobolt and Bojan Dekleva highlighting the link between the theory and practice of contemporary developments in child and youth social care and educational practice in Slovenia, within a European context. These trends can be described as expanding the goals, method and models of work with service users. Although based on the example of Slovenia, the chapter's argument that 'the achieved level of professionalisation calls for further development to enhance the higher quality of practice' can be seen as transferable.

Extrafamilial care is also at centre of both the following articles from Kaija Klap and Emmanuel Grupper and Irit Mero-Jaffe. Kaija Klap deals with the essential role of family relations in a child's development and the difficulties parents may have in parenting. She maintains that these perspectives are important to consider when the child is growing up in extrafamilial care. Another aspect deals with the working model, including the methods in Lauste Family Rehabilitation Centre in Finland and especially the family's role in the child's upbringing and treatment process. To help blunt the parent-child conflicts inherent in the dual loyalties faced by children towards their parents and towards the residential group home and to improve the relationship between them and their parents as well as with the group home staff are the goals of the project discussed by Emmanuel Grupper and Irit Mero-Jaffe.

Since participation matters in both the above approaches, it is not by chance that participation projects complete this book. Mechthild Wolff reports from a practice development project which took place within a bigger project on quality for children. Her observations make clear that participation is not only a question of quality but also an expression of the civil rights and the citizen status of children and young people. This overall effort to strengthen the civil rights of children and young people is the background for her account of the participation of children and youth in residential child care in Germany. From the Netherlands Marc Noom and Micha de Winter describe a most unusual kind of participatory practice: they examine the perceptions of homeless youth about the care they receive by involving homeless youth as participants in their project through adopting peer-research. Peer-research is a specific form of collaborative research, and gives a major role to the homeless youth in making an inventory of the problems. In the discussion a parallel is drawn between the parent-adolescent relationship and the relationship between the social worker and the homeless adolescent.

References

Beck, U and Bonß, W, eds (1989) *Weder Sozialtechnologie noch Aufklärung? Analysen zur Verwendung sozialwissenschaftlichen Wissens* Frankfurt/Main, Suhrkamp

Beker, J and Schwartz, I (1994) Does institutional care do more harm than good? In Gambrill, E and Stein, T J, eds, *Controversial Issues in Child Welfare*, p275-289 London, Allyn and Bacon

Besley, A C (2006) Governmentality, neoliberalism, and the professionalisation of school counselling. In Weber, S and Maurer, S, eds, *Gouvernementalität und Erziehungswissenschaft: Wissen – Macht – Transformation*, p181-196 Wiesbaden, VS Verlag für Sozialwissenschaften

Bettelheim, B (1950) *Love is Not Enough* New York, Free Press

Bettelheim, B (1974) A Home for the Heart London, Thames and Hudson

Bourdieu, P (1994) Der Habitus als Vermittlung zwischen Struktur und Praxis. In Bourdieu, P, ed, *Zur Soziologie der symbolischen Formen*, p125-159 Frankfurt/Main, Suhrkamp Translated by Wolfgang Fietkau

Bowlby, E J M (1953) *Child Care and the Growth of Love: based by permission of the World Health Organization on the report 'Maternal Care and Mental Health'*. Abridged and edited by Margery Fry London, Penguin

Cullen, F T and Gendreau, P (2001) From nothing works to what works: changing professional ideology in the 21st century *The Prison Journal*, 81:313-338

Davies, M (2000) Nothing works. In Davies, M, ed, *The Blackwell Encyclopaedia of Social Work* Oxford, Blackwell Publishers

Department for Education and Skills (2006) *Care Matters: transforming the Lives of Children and Young People in Care* Cm 6932 London, The Stationery Office

Dewe, B, Ferchhoff, W, and Radtke, F O (1992) Das Professionswissen von Pädagogen Ein wissenstheoretischer Rekonstruktionsversuch. In Dewe, B, ed, *Erziehen als Profession: Zur Logik professionellen Handelns in pädagogischen Feldern,* p70-91 Opladen, Leske und Budrich

Dewe, B, Ferchoff, W, Scherr, A, and Stüwe, G (1993) *Professionelles soziales Handeln: soziale Arbeit im Spannungsfeld zwischen Theorie und Praxis* Weinheim; München, Juventa-Verlag

Dewe, B and Otto, H-U (2002) Reflexive Sozialpädagogik Grundstrukturen eines neuen Typs dienstleistungsorientierten Professionshandelns. In Thole, W, ed, *Grundriss Soziale Arbeit: ein einführendes Handbuch*, p179-198 Opladen, Leske und Budrich

Fisher, M (2005) Knowledge production for social welfare: enhancing the evidence base. In Sommerfeld, P, ed, *Evidence-Based Social Work: towards a New Professionalism?*, p127-147 Bern; New York, Peter Lang

Foucault, M (1979a) *The History of Sexuality*, Volume 1 London, Allen Lane

Foucault, M (1979b) On governmentality *Ideology and Consciousness,* (6):5-21

Friedman, M (1962) *Capitalism and Freedom* London, Chicago University Press

Gira, E C, Kessler, M L, and Poertner, J (2004) Influencing social workers to use research evidence in practice: lessons from medicine and the allied health professions *Research on Social Work Practice*, 14(2):68-79

Goffman, E (1968) *Asylums: Essays on the Social Situation of Mental Patients and Other Inmates* Harmondsworth, Penguin

Gredig, D (2005) The co-evolution of knowledge production and transfer evidence-based intervention development as an approach to improve the impact of evidence on social work. In Sommerfeld, P, ed, *Evidence-Based Social Work: towards a New Professionalism?*, p173-198 Bern; New York, Peter Lang

Habermas, J (1990) *Moral Consciousness and Communicative Action* Cambridge, Polity

Hamberger, M, Koch, J, Peters, F, and Treptow, R, eds (2006) *Children at risk – Kinder- und Jugendhilfe in Mittel- und Osteuropa* Frankfurt/Main, Internationale Gesellschaft für Erzieherische Hilfe

Hansbauer, P (2008) Structural dynamics in society and innovations in the German residential care child system, in this book

Hayeck, F A von (1944) *The Road to Serfdom* London, George Routledge

Hornstein, W (1998) Erziehungswissenschaftliche Forschung und Sozialpädagogik. In Rauschenbach, T and Thole, W, eds, *Sozialpädagogische Forschung Gegenstand und Funktionen, Bereiche und Methoden*, p47-80 Weinheim; München, Juventa-Verlag

Kahan, B (1994) *Growing up in groups* London, Her Majesty's Stationery Office

Kaufmann, F X (1976) Zur Problematik der Effektivität und ihrer Erfassung im Bereich der sozialen Sicherung In Külp, B and Haas, H-D, eds, *Soziale Probleme der modernen Industriegesellschaft*, p489-517 Berlin, Duncker und Humblot

Kobolt, A and Dekleva, B (2008) The professionalisation of child and youth care practice: professionalising social pedagogy from practice to theory and back to practice, in this book

Luhmann, N and Schorr, K E (1982) Das Technologiedefizit der Erziehung und die Pädagogik In Luhmann, N and Schorr, K E, eds, *Zwischen Technologie und Selbstreferenz*, p11-40 Frankfurt/Main, Suhrkamp

Millham, S, Bullock, R, and Hosie, K (1978) *Locking up Children: secure provision within the child care system* Farnborough, Saxon House

Mollenhauer, K (1972) *Theorien zum Erziehungsprozess: zur Einf. in erziehungswissenschaftl Fragestellungen* München, Juventa-Verlag

Otto, H-U and Schnurr, S, eds (2000) *Privatisierung und Wettbewerb in der Jugendhilfe: marktorientierte Modernisierungsstrategien in internationaler Perspektive* Neuwied; Kriftel, Luchterhand

Peters, F (2004) Qualitätsentwicklung unter den Bedingungen von Markt und Wettbewerb In Beckmann, C, Otto, H-U, Richter, M, and Schrödter, M, eds, *Qualität in der Sozialen Arbeit: zwischen Nutzerinteresse und Kostenkontrolle*, p155-171 Wiesbaden, VS Verlag für Sozialwissenschaften

Peters, F (2006a) Hilfen zur Erziehung im Kontext von (sozial-)staatlichen Modernisierungsstrategien im europäischen Vergleich (im Erscheinen)

Peters, F (2006b) Wirkungsorientierte Steuerung? Eine kritische Betrachtung In Gintzel, U and Drößler, T, eds, *Vom Eigensinn sozialpädagogischer Fachlichkeit: Qualität in den Hilfen zur Erziehung*, p183-220 Aachen, Shaker

Peters, M (1999) Neo-liberalism. In Peters, M, Ghiradelli, P Jr, Standish, P, and Zarnic, B, eds, *Encyclopaedia of Philosophy of Education* htpp://wwwvussthr/ENCYCLOPAEDIA/

Peters, M A (2001) *Poststructuralism, Marxism, and neoliberalism: Between Theory and Politics* Oxford, Rowman and Littlefield

Petrie, P, Boddy, J, Cameron, C, Heptinstall, E, McQuail, S, and Wigfall, V (2003) Working with children: social pedagogy and residential child care in Europe Unpublished Report to the Department of Health

Redl, F (1966) *When we deal with children: selected writings* London, Collier-Macmillan

Rubington, E and Weinberg, M S, eds (1968) *Deviance. The Interactionist Perspective. Texts and readings in the Sociology of Deviance* London, Collier-Macmillan

Sackett, D L, Rosenberg, W M, Gray, M J A, Haynes, B R, and Richardson, S W (1996) Evidence based medicine: what it is and what it isn't *British Medical Journal*, (312):7172

Schön, D A (1987) *Educating the reflective practitioner* London, Jossey Bass

Schur, E M (1973) *Radical Non-Intervention. Rethinking The Delinquency Problem* Englewood Cliffs, Prentice Hall

Shaw, I (2005) Evidencing social work In Sommerfeld, P, ed, *Evidence-Based Social Work: towards a New Professionalism?*, p73-107 Bern; New York, Peter Lang

Sommerfeld, P, ed (2005) *Evidence-Based Social Work: towards a New Professionalism?* Bern; New York, Peter Lang

Sommerfeld, P, Hollenstein, L, Calzaferri, R, and Schiepek, G (2005) Realtime monitoring: new methods for evidence-based social work. In Sommerfeld, P, ed, *Evidence-Based Social Work: towards a New Professionalism?*, p199-232 Bern; New York, Peter Lang

Sumner, C (1990) *Censure, Politics And Criminal Justice* Milton Keynes, Open University Press

Thiersch, H and Rauschenbach, T (1984) Sozialpädagogik/Sozialarbeit: Theorie und Entwicklung. In Eyferth, H, ed, *Handbuch Sozialarbeit, Sozialpädagogik*, p984-1016 Darmstadt; Neuwied, Luchterhand

Trede, W (2008) Residential child care in European countries: recent trends, in this book

Walter, I, Nutley, S, Percy-Smith, J, McNeish, D, and Frost, S (2004) Improving the use of research in social care practice *Knowledge Review* 7 London, Social Care Institute for Excellence

White, V (2003) Drei Modi des Managements sozialer Arbeit Entwicklungen in Großbritannien In Dahme, H-J, Otto, H-U, Trube, A, and Wohlfahrt, N, eds, *Soziale Arbeit für den aktivierenden Staat*, p419435 Leverkusen, Leske und Budrich

Wichern, J H (1964) *Schriften zur Sozialpädagogik* Bad Heilbrunn/Obb, Klinkhardt

Ziegler, H (2005) What works in social work challenging the political agenda. In Sommerfeld, P, ed, *Evidence-Based Social Work: towards a New Professionalism?*, p31-52 Bern; New York, Peter Lang

2

Residential child care in European
countries: Recent trends

Wolfgang Trede

Introduction

Since the 1970s there has been a great deal of reform to modernise youth welfare and the field of residential child care. In consequence there have been considerable forces for change in this field which present difficulties in speaking about residential care, because there is not one form of institutional upbringing, but a great many. When considering residential care, it is necessary to speak about it in the plural or perhaps use a pedagogical systematic concept such as 'upbringing in another place' (*Erziehung an einem anderen Ort*) (Trede and Winkler, 2000). This definition applies just as widely in the Anglo-Saxon world; as Milham and his colleagues put it, 'The only feature that characterises residential settings is the 'bed' which is not provided by the family but by others' (Millham *et al*, 1986, p8).

The placement and education of children and adolescents in residential care homes is, unless it is only a short-term measure, certainly one of the most powerful forms of youth welfare affecting young people's life histories – even if the institutional setting has been adapted to provide a milieu suited to individual needs.

So child and youth care today can take the following forms (Trede and Winkler, 2000):

group education, although sometimes still provided in large building complexes, involves a more familial style in which small groups of 6 to 10 children, mostly made up of both sexes (but sometimes only girls) form groups which are autonomous in most aspects of everyday life. The children are looked after around the clock by a team of educators or social pedagogues, who are responsible for providing a good upbringing, for ensuring good relationships among the group members and between them and the staff, for their educational progress and their emotional feelings as well as for considering their long-term needs. They usually work with the families of the children in one way or another, to strengthen their capabilities, because nearly always the aim is for the children to go back to their parents or families once the home conditions become more suitable. Otherwise there is the option to stay until the age of 18 or even longer to enable them to stay on at school or try to get vocational qualifications.

therapeutic education emphasises some kind of specific therapeutic milieu or uses some kind of behaviour therapy although only a minority of these facilities work strictly in accordance with a particular therapeutic school

family education care, which is professionally based, provides everyday care. Following criticism of large facilities, children's homes and other small facilities have been developed, often run by private providers. For example, an educator couple may live with up to five children in a home of their own, sometimes with their own children and sometimes not. This setting is very close to 'treatment foster caring' (*Erziehungsstellen*).

independent living in which a young person lives in a flat rented from the provider of this service, either alone or in a twosome. It is sometimes used as a transition from the living group to autonomous status as well as in very specific circumstances. The social and pedagogical assistance in this setting is organised in response to the needs and demands of the youngster and may vary from close support to loose links with a social worker or pedagogue.

flexible care or forms of individualised care which fall between residential care and street-work, including drop-in centres or direct access accommodation, often serve youngsters who avoid other approaches, who have left their families or who live in problematic or deviant situations where they experience things such as homelessness, prostitution, and drug abuse. Flexible care may be highly individualised to match the varying needs of adolescents without being linked to a particular kind of housing or residential living. The question of where and how he or she should settle down is left open and is dependent upon the interaction process.

adventure-based care tries to build up new relationships between adults and young people through confrontation with foreign cultures and in foreign regions or through sharing new experiences such as sailing and climbing. Such arrangements are also intended to shape the character and broaden the mind and some include some kind of formal education, like the Danish model of 'travelling schools' (Tvind Schools) (Ziehe and Stubenrauch, 1982).

crisis-centres include shelters for underage girls or women, centres for underage and unsupervised refugees, and vocational training centres

All these – and possibly other – arrangements are found in residential care not only in Germany, which over the years has changed from a tradition of institutional upbringing towards offering some kind of professional assisted socialisation and education.

But there are difficulties:

- The factual plurality of the care settings which can be categorised under residential child care in current practice complicates generalising statements even for one country.

- The problems of defining the subject matter in international comparisons are even greater because residential child care has to be distinguished from neighbouring fields such as full-time care, (special) boarding schools, facilities for disabled children and youth prisons whose inclusion or exclusion may result in false comparisons.

- There is hardly any up-to-date data or systematic knowledge to enable international comparisons and generalisations. The available country reports are based upon data from the eighties and the beginning of the nineties (Gottesmann, 1991; Colton and Hellinckx, 1993; Gottesmann, 1994; Colla, 1999).

All in all, therefore, the following remarks are at best exploratory. They are in two parts:

1. a survey of various national policies concerning placement outside a family, that is to say, the totality of the aims and programmes as well as the actual actions of relevant societal agencies – the governments, public and private agencies and associations – relating to the extra-familial placement of children and adolescents and

2. some data about the population, the reasons for children entering care and the duration of residential child care. (Trede, 1999a,b)

The status of residential child care in Europe

In the more developed European countries, particularly within the European Union, there is the stated belief that placements outside the family in institutional education should be avoided as far as possible. This means all short, medium and long-term placements in the context of public education.

For the five countries I investigated at the end of the nineties – Germany, England, Finland, Poland, and Slovenia – this policy was realised to only a limited extent with respect to the actual numbers of placements. Comparing the number of minors per one thousand of the peer population placed outside their own family in homes, supported accommodation sheltered housing, foster families and other placements during the decade 1985 to 1995, in all the countries except England, the numbers were seen to be unchanged. In Germany and Finland, which only have a very limited number of placements outside the family, the percentage was rising, despite obviously improved preventive assistance. Only in England could one identify a decline in the totals quoted from 4.6 per cent to 3.4 per cent. The number of institutional placements here decreased from 20,090 minors living in homes in 1985 to 8,790 in 1995, a notable reduction in the percentage of placements outside the family from 1.68 per cent to 0.75 per cent.

However, this enormous drop by more than a half may be due to substitution effects. Residential child care had a particularly bad image in England and it had been shaken by several scandals in the last decade, mainly violence and sexual abuse on the part of educators against children and adolescents, which even occupied parliamentary investigation committees. Instead of being placed in children's homes, which were poorly thought of, children and adolescents may have increasingly been placed in special boarding schools which are not included in the statistics for children's homes (Kahan, 1991).

Nonetheless, it is extremely difficult to identify which factors were responsible for the increase in Germany and Finland of extrafamilial placements and what weight they carried. The rising demand in Germany may have been a consequence of increasing psycho-social problems because of rising poverty, high unemployment and increasingly fragile family constellations among other things. A study in south-west Germany (Württemberg-Hohenzollern), which examined the reasons for the regionally varied utilisation of residential child care, supports this interpretation. According to this study, socio-structural factors (the number of minor social benefit recipients, the unemployment rate and population density among other things) significantly affect the demand of placements outside the family (Ames and Bürger, 1998). At least for the region investigated this means that the efforts to avoid placements outside the family were probably effective but they were over-compensated by socio-structural factors.

Several other factors have also to be considered to assess country-specific developments: the rising number may be due to the increased 'discovery' of demands because of a more widely available and accessible support system, and a changed and more service orientated understanding of youth welfare. Also new youth welfare laws can create new benefits – thinking only of the extension of benefits for over-eighteens in the German Child and Youth Services Act. Finally, the social-administrative and political processes of organising and defining may play a role (Bürger *et al*, 1994).

So we see that different cultures concerning placement outside the family exist in Europe, and that the intention to avoid institutional education and full-time care is, at least until now, not reflected in the actual numbers. How then do the countries under consideration refer to homes and related institutional arrangements in comparison with full-time care in families?

Differences between the countries are clear. In England and Slovenia more than 75 per cent of placements outside the family are in foster families, and in Finland full-time family care, at approximately 58 per cent, is also the dominant form of children's placements. But Germany and Poland have a preponderance of residential child care. It is especially remarkable that Germany is the only European country (Colton and Hellinckx, 1993; Madge, 1994) in which there was no increase of the foster family proportion in placements outside the family over the decade. Everywhere in Europe except Germany the emphasis is on foster families.

Several countries have a significantly lower percentages of foster family placements for traditional reasons: less than 3 per cent in Greece, 14 per cent in Spain, and 27 per cent in Italy. Only in Germany is there no policy of putting foster families first, and this can be explained by

1. the lack of a strong and clear youth welfare policy – foster families in Germany are more utilised than appreciated and seriously promoted

2. the strong position of parental custody in the German youth welfare legislation and the anxiety of parents over the placement of their child in a rival family, which they fantasise as being 'better,' which are obstacles to placing a child in a foster family

3. children's homes having proved reform-friendly throughout the last 25 years and being seen to be a highly professional alternative to the classical foster family, that is, in the form of group homes or in settings similar to treatment foster care and in intensive work with parents.

Germany, then, has comparatively high numbers of placements outside the family, which means that compared with other countries in Europe, a high proportion of minors is temporarily or permanently placed outside their own families. And it relies less on foster families and more on an institutional professional system of placements outside the family.

Trends within European residential child care

The clientele of residential child care, from all that is known, scarcely differs across Europe. Residential education and care is firstly a service for children from socially disadvantaged families, usually with an accumulation of economic, social, psychological and health problems (Gottesmann, 1991; Madge, 1994). Children and adolescents come predominantly from difficult family situations, influenced by cramped housing, unemployment, reliance on social benefits and so on. In many countries the children of ethnic minorities, from single parent and step families are also disproportionately involved. It is reported that a high percentage of children have experienced violence and that alcohol and drug problems exist in many families.

Age of the clientele

We see a general trend to place younger children in foster families if possible, and older children more frequently in residential homes. However, there are fairly distinct differences between the countries. In Germany, for example, approximately 35 per cent of the residential population is aged between 15 and 18, whereas in Sweden and in the Netherlands almost three quarters of those living in a home belong to the somewhat bigger age group of those aged 14 to 18. In Germany at the end of 1995 nearly 12 per cent of the home population was up to 9 years old, in Slovenia the proportion of the under-10-year-old home children was 2 per cent, because state guidelines forbid any child under 6 years to be placed in a home. By contrast, the relatively large number of younger children in German homes almost exclusively live in family-like small homes or children's villages, where they grow up in a supportive setting.

Duration of residential care

The time children spend in of residential care is decreasing in European countries. This is due to the professional view that institutional education should be planned as a short-term intervention with the goal of returning children to the family as soon as possible, as well as the increasing economic pressure everywhere to limit the length of expensive institutional placements. Of the young people who completed a residential placement in 1998 in Germany, approximately 37 per cent had been staying up to 12 months in these homes, 20 per cent spent between 1 and 2 years in a home, and 14 per cent had been living there for 5 years. The average duration of an institutional placement in Germany in 1998 was 29 months (Statistisches Bundesamt, 2000).

In many European countries, however, placements are shorter. To give an extreme example, in England the average stay in 1997-1998 lasted only 7 months! Approximately 40 per cent of placements lasted less than a month, and only 4 per cent lasted over two years. It is interesting that placements in foster families were similarly short-lived.

These data, however, refer only to completed placements, so say nothing about the whole youth welfare career of an adolescent. The assumption that English children have to experience shorter placements outside the family more often is confirmed by a national directive issued by the English Department of Health, the responsible authority for institutional education at national level. The 'National Priorities Guidance' addressed each local authority, stating, 'Until 2001 the proportion of children looked after, who within a year had three placements and more, is to be reduced to maximum 16 per cent.' (Social Services Inspectorate, 1998). The guidance indicates an important general condition of English welfare, namely its centralist nature, but the placement system is significantly different from that in Germany, Belgium, France and Luxembourg. Children's homes, along with foster families, facing these short stays seem to be transitional or crisis cushioning places, possibly homes 'around the corner' and so almost part of the social infrastructure, on which children can fall back – even repeatedly – for limited periods.

Developments in youth services law

In the European comparison, common grounds in law are noteworthy at two levels. First, the child and youth service laws passed in Europe during the last decade are determined by the UN Convention on the Rights of the Child. Closely based on the Convention, educational services provide counselling, participatory and hearing rights for minors, special rights of protection in institutions, and in some countries rights to complain (as in England and the Netherlands) as well as special representational instruments (as for instance the children and youth lawyers in Austria). Secondly, there are corresponding organisational forms of educational services, which, following widely shared similar policies, aim to provide environmentally friendly institutional settings close to the children's home areas.

However, there are clear distinctions in the fundamental orientations of public professional educational actions between English, Finnish and

German laws, with their strong family orientation on the one hand, and Polish regulations with their orientation towards statutory monitoring, carried out by professionals, on the other. Even if both patterns refer in their basic statements to 'the child's well-being', the Polish legislation – shown in international comparison as certainly not unique – derives from the fact that statement of the 'best interest of the child' and consequently the definition of endangering situations have to be made by specialists, while other countries' laws take account of empirical research (Millham *et al*, 1986) and have a sceptical attitude towards an 'expertocracy', based on a new self-restraint and on negotiation processes between professionals and service users (Merchel, 1999).

If, however, one considers the status of minors placed outside the family, specifically the extent of placements against the will of parents, you can see that, for example in England now as ever, the majority of placement cases – 57 per cent in 1995 – are preceded by the decision of the family court which replaces parental rights fully or partially. This, at least *prima facie*, is contrary to the Children Act 1989 of England and Wales, which put greater emphasis on partnership and voluntary collaboration. In Finland the proportion of children and adolescents placed against the will of their parents has also increased in the last decade (Kemppainen, 1994), as it has in Germany where, in the last few years, the proportion of cases involving the newly introduced educational assistance in homes and foster families which were preceded by a withdrawal of custody also rose, but only slightly, amounting to 15 per cent in 1998 (Statistisches Bundesamt, 2000).

This paradoxical development can be taken to indicate that a service-oriented youth welfare system is compelled more quickly to choose the judicial way in problem situations which have to be professionally assessed as seriously endangering. Additionally, acute incidents and subsequent expert debates (as for example after the death of two neglected foster children near Stuttgart some years ago) can raise the sensibility of social workers regarding their 'guarantors' position' and their legal responsibility, and so can lead to a speedier involvement of the guardianship court.

Making children strong

In the context of developments in child and youth services law, the UN Convention on the Rights of the Child had enormous effect in encouraging an improvement in international standards in the field of children's rights. It led to sustainable sensitising concepts in professional social work. Rights of information, participation, and hearing and/or complaint systems were integrated into national laws. The UN Convention on the Rights of the Child contributed to the replacement of the formerly dominant 'protection and control' paradigm by a partnership-based 'assistance' concept, or to shifts in its direction. It is beyond the scope of this chapter to compare developments in Europe with regard to the respect of children's rights in residential homes. The indicators listed below are only those examined in the international comparison I am reporting here.

1. How comprehensively and adequately are children, adolescents and parents informed, for example, about the national youth welfare law, about important procedures, for instance in the planning of services, about possible forms of assistance or complaint options?

2. How comprehensively and adequately can young people and parents participate in decisions and the assistance processes, for example home councils in Hessen, and participatory seminars (Blandow *et al*, 1999)?

3. Which actual, subjective rights do children and adolescents have in their respective youth welfare systems? Which age limits exist concerning this, for example in Germany the right to advice, the right to be taken into care?

4. What options are there for complaints in the respective system, such as complaints procedures in England/Wales and the Netherlands?

5. Are there self-help groups of young people, such as 'Who cares?' in Scotland, comparable active and state-supported self-help groups in the Netherlands and in Finland?

An example will illustrate how differently the right to information is handled in practice. In Germany the right to information or, even more, the obligation to provide comprehensive information is written into the Child and Youth Services Act, but this is rarely put into practice. So there is scant information material suitable for young people in Germany except one or two brochures produced by the Protestant Educational Association and by the IGfH publishing company, compared with other countries such as Scotland. In Scotland there is a range of information brochures suitable for children and adolescents, for instance about the 'Children's Hearings'. The respect of children's rights is also visible in the National Care Standards enacted in 2002 by the Scottish Government. Their goal is to guarantee good care standards ('Safe Caring for Children and Young Persons'), developed according to the perspective of young people. The brochure 'National Care Standards' addresses children and adolescents especially. Standard 1, for example, says, 'You are welcome in the home and you know what you may expect during your stay. You are given the feeling of being welcomed. You and your family will receive good, up-to-date information about the home from a flyer or an information set, which is written in colloquial English or in a language and way, suitable for you ... ' This seems to be an example of best practice from which we can certainly learn!

Résumé

Faced with the conceptual and legal similarities of different countries, it is astonishing how different the systems are. Significantly different are:

- the qualification level of the staff members and the relations between clients and workers (Trede, 1999)

- their attitude and practice in relation to children's rights and participation

- the duration of institutional placements.

My investigation is based on the available material on country-specific residential child care cultures. There is an urgent need for qualitatively conceptualised comparative field studies which in particular reconstruct the perspective of the children and young people receiving the services.

References

Ames, A and Bürger, U (1998) *Untersuchung der Ursachen der unter schiedlichen Inanspruchnahme vollstationärer Heimerziehung im Verbandsgebiet* Stuttgart, Landeswohlfahrtsverband Württemberg-Hohenzollern, Landesjugendamt

Blandow, J, Gintzel, U, and Hansbauer, P (1999) *Partizipation als Qualitätsmerkmal in der Heimerziehung: Eine Diskussionsgrundlage* Münster, Votum

Bürger, U, Lehning, K, and Seidenstücker, B (1994) *Heimunterbringungsentwicklung in der Bundesrepublik Deutschland Theoretischer Zugang, Datenlage und Hypothesen* Frankfurt/Main, ISS Gemeinnütziger e.V.

Colla, H E, ed (1999) *Handbuch Heimerziehung und Pflegekinderwesen in Europa* Neuwied; Kriftel, Luchterhand

Colton, M J and Hellinckx, W, eds (1993) *Child Care in the EC: A Country-Specific Guide to Foster and Residential Care* Aldershot, Arena

Gottesmann, M, ed (1991) *Residential Child Care: An International Reader* London, Whiting and Birch, SCA Education series No 1

Gottesmann, M, ed (1994) *Recent Changes and New Trends in Extrafamilial Child Care: An International Perspective* London, Whiting and Birch

Kahan, B (1991) Residential care and education in Great Britain. In Gottesmann, M, ed, *Residential Child Care: An International Reader*, p138-156 London, Whiting and Birch, SCA Education series No 1

Kemppainen, M (1994) Trends in Finnish child welfare. In Gottesmann, M, ed, *Recent Changes and New Trends in Extrafamilial Child Care: An International Perspective*, p39-46 London, Whiting and Birch

Madge, N (1994) *Children and Residential Care in Europe* London, National Children's Bureau

Merchel, J (1999) Zwischen 'Diagnose' und 'Aushandlung' Zum Verständnis des Charakters von Hilfeplanung in der Erziehungshilfe. In Peters, F, ed, *Diagnosen – Gutachten – hermeneutisches Fallverstehen Rekonstruktive Verfahren zur Qualifizierung individueller Hilfeplanung*, p73-96 Regensburg,Walhalla-Fachverlag, Internationale Gesellschaft für Erzieherische Hilfen

Millham, S, Bullock, R, Hosie, K, and Haak, M (1986) Lost in Care Aldershot, Gower

Social Services Inspectorate (1998) *Someone else's children: inspections of planning and decision making for children looked after and the safety of children looked after* London, Department of Health

Statistisches Bundesamt (2000) *Fachserie 13, Reihe 6.1.2-3 Jugendhilfe Erzieherische Hilfen außerhalb des Elternhauses* Wiesbaden, Statistisches Bundesamt

Trede, W (1999a) Heimerziehung als Beruf – Die Situation in Europa. In Colla, H E, ed, *Handbuch Heimerziehung und Pflegekinderwesen in Europa* p801-811 Neuwied; Kriftel, Luchterhand

Trede, W (1999b) Konzepte der Heimerziehung im europäischen Vergleich. In Fatke, R, ed, *Erziehung und sozialer Wandel: Brennpunkte sozialpädagogischer Forschung, Theoriebildung und Praxis*, p318-338 Weinheim; Basel, Beltz, Zeitschrift für Pädagogik: Beiheft; 39

Trede, W and Winkler, M (2000) Stationäre Erziehungshilfen: Heim, Wohngruppe, Pflegefamilie. In Krüger, H H and Rauschenbach, T, eds, *Einführung in die Arbeitsfelder des Bildungs- und Sozialwesens: Einführungskurs Erziehungswissenschaft IV*, p251-268 Wiesbaden, VS Verlag für Sozialwissenschaften

Ziehe, T and Stubenrauch, H (1982) *Plädoyer für ungewöhnliches Lernen* Reinbek bei Hamburg, Rowohlt

3

Residential communities
as a secure base

Keith J. White

Introduction

One of the most important influences on our current understanding of child development is the attachment theory introduced by Dr John Bowlby. He presented studies of the detrimental effects of maternal deprivation on young children in a World Health Organisation Report, *Maternal Care and Mental Health* (1952). This became widely known through its summary, *Child Care and the Growth of Love* (1953). The essence of his argument is that mental health depends on satisfactory ('good enough' would be Winnicott's term) parenting of very young children and that at the heart of this relationship is a form of emotional bonding or attachment.

Until Bowlby's intervention the focus of attention had been largely on the physical, social and medical conditions and environment of the child. A good substitute setting for a child – whether foster care or children's home – was seen as better than a poverty-stricken, dysfunctional family in a neighbourhood beset with health problems. In the second half of the twentieth century another mantra was coined: 'a poor home is better than a good institution'. And 'institutional' care, though still common worldwide, continues to be seen as a last resort.

The chapter reviews residential care and its functions in the light of the aspect of Bowlby's work which he continued to stress increasingly right to his last work, *A Secure Base* (1988). The argument of the chapter is that, contrary to popular professional assumptions and policies, residential care has in the past provided many children with a secure base in the sense that Bowlby meant it, and that such care continues to offer the possibility of this core element of parenting, given the right conditions.

A secure base

We can let John Bowlby speak for himself,

> A central feature of my concept of parenting (is) the provision by both parents of a secure base from which a child or an adolescent can make sorties into the outside world and to which he can return knowing for sure that he will be welcomed when he gets there, nourished physically and emotionally, comforted if distressed, reassured if frightened. In essence this role is one of being available, ready to respond when called upon to encourage and perhaps assist, but to intervene actively only when clearly necessary. (Bowlby, 1988, p11)

Later in this collection of papers Bowlby writes of five therapeutic tasks of which the provision of a secure base is the first, '...a secure base from which he can explore the various unhappy and painful aspects of his life, past and present, many of which he finds it difficult or perhaps impossible to think about and reconsider without a trusted companion to provide support, encouragement, sympathy, and, on occasion, guidance' (Bowlby, 1988, p138).

At the outset of his research and theory Bowlby, controversially, saw the mother as the primary potential provider of a secure base through bonding and attachment. But as his work developed he came to see how the process of parenting and the formation of attachments were neither restricted to the very young child nor to the mother. So it is possible for a therapist to be the one who provides a secure base for a person who has not known one consistently before. He puts it like this,

> The therapeutic alliance appears as a secure base, an internal object as a working, or representational, model of an attachment figure, reconstruction as exploring memories of the past, resistance (sometimes) as deep reluctance to disobey the past orders of parents not to tell or not to remember. In the foregoing description the therapist's role has been likened to that of a mother who provides her child with a secure base from which to explore. This means, first and foremost, that he accepts and respects his patient, warts and all, as a fellow human being in trouble and that his over-riding concern is to promote his patient's welfare by all means at his disposal. To this end the therapist strives to be reliable, attentive, empathic, and sympathetically responsive, and also to encourage his patient to explore the world of his thoughts, feelings, and actions not only in the present but also in the past. (Bowlby, 1988, pp151-152)

One aspect of the interpretation of attachment theory that has dogged its development and application has been a concern that attachment is linked to dependence. This carries with it the adverse connotation that it is associated with the early years and that one ought to grow out of it. Thus when attachment behaviour is manifested in later years it has been regarded as regrettable or even regressive. Bowlby comments, 'I believe that to be an appalling misjudgement' (Bowlby, 1988, p12). Strong words from a researcher usually meticulous in his phrasing and judgements!

So in summary, according to Bowlby, sound attachments, and a secure base as a core element of them, develop normally and ideally between a child and his biological parents, and are vital for mental health in growing children and adults, but such attachments can to some degree develop in other settings and contexts throughout life. However detrimental a poor mother-child bonding may be, it is not necessarily the end of the story.

Residential child care

Somewhere along the line residential child care got a very bad name. The ideal setting for a child is the child's biological family, so social policies were directed to supporting and maintaining that setting. If this proved impossible, the best alternative was something as like the archetypal family as possible: adoption or foster care. Residential care was seen as institutional, and in many respects the very opposite of what a child needs. I developed this analysis in a paper, *The Ideology of Residential Care and Fostering* (White, 2002).

If we put on one side the very poor forms of residential care, together with the very poor family, adoptive and foster care settings, the question arises as to whether residential child care can provide positive experiences of attachment for children and young people which could be described as a secure base. For reasons outlined, the prevailing ideology and policy makers will not countenance this question. To them it is axiomatic that residential care can never do this. Around the world they make it their primary task to advocate every other form of care except residential care.

But let us stay with the question in an open and enquiring way. What evidence do we have?

First, is there anything essential to residential child care that prevents it serving the functions and processes that Bowlby describes?

Second, what are the reflections and views of children and young people themselves in residential establishments?

Third, what are the lifelong experiences of those who lived in residential care fifty or more years ago?

Fourth, what is the experience of our residential community at Mill Grove over more than a century?

This is by no means an exhaustive list of options, but it does provide substantive material for any who are open-minded enough to consider the matter fairly.

Residential child care and the provision of a secure base

Speaking as someone who is neither partisan nor committed to the inherent supremacy of one form of child care over all others, I cannot see how residential child care can be better portrayed than in the way Bowlby describes the therapeutic relationship and task. This is what establishments are committed to, and this is what happens when the process is working well. I have pondered each of the words and phrases quoted from Bowlby's work and hope that there will, in future, be conscious echoes of it in the vision statements of residential communities and the specifications of the work, responsibilities and personalities of staff and team members.

Acceptance and respect are surely the *sine qua non* of residential child care, and staff are chosen because they are reliable, attentive, empathic, sympathetic in their approach to those whom they serve, and seek to help a person or persons explore thoughts, feelings and actions past and present.

It is clearly true for numerous reasons, including lack of resources, poor training and leadership, poor management, wrong settings, and poor recruitment of staff, that residential care has not provided such people, or such an approach, but there is absolutely nothing inherent about residential child care that militates against what Bowlby is advocating, and everything inherent that aspires to exactly this set of goals and processes.

The views of young people

Over the past couple of decades there has been a steady trickle of research in the UK describing the views of children and young people about residential and foster care. I summarised one such study (White, 2002, p234) and Ian Milligan (2006) at the Scottish Institute for Residential Child Care has done similar work.

Two things stand out: first, that some young people often and consistently express a preference for residential care over foster care and alternatives; second, that this always surprises the policy makers and media. Why do the young people express this preference? It would be useful to have more information on this, but my findings are that some had experienced safe, reliable, stable and predictable care; that the adults caring for them had been reliable and resourceful friends, and that some of the other residents had also become good friends. They had found a safe, non-threatening environment. Whereas foster care is marked by expectations of how they should see and relate to adults, and a high degree of placement breakdown, residential care, despite its high staff turnover, is still seen as relatively flexible and reliable.

As for the constant surprise of the policymakers and media, it surely demonstrates that they are not taking the views of young people seriously. As Thomas Kuhn (1962) pointed out, science does not proceed simply on the basis of objective experimentation and data but operates within paradigms. It takes more than evidence to shift a paradigm, and it will take an awful lot of pushing to shift the current attachment to the ideals of family and foster care.

The experiences of those in care many decades ago

I have not done a systematic study, but it has been my privilege to have talked with many people who lived in homes run by Barnardo's and other voluntary organisations when they were children. One of the recurrent themes has been that they were provided with a secure base. It may not have been ideal, but it gave them a start in life, and a foundation on which to build. They talk fondly of the communal life of the village and other settings.

I accept that there is an element of wishful thinking, and something of a golden glow about these memories. But the fact is that these people believe they were given a secure base, and surely this belief is an important element of what constitutes such a base. They have explored life from that base, and it remains important in their minds. Barnardo's has long since sought to shrug off the label 'Barnardo's family' but it is not easily discarded when so many former residents choose it as their preferred option.

There are those who have written about the abuse and neglect they suffered while in residential care, and I take this seriously. But such stories have been written about biological families and foster care settings as well. My point is that the existence of so many people who see residential care positively cannot be disregarded without careful consideration.

The experience of Mill Grove

This leads me finally to the experience of Mill Grove, the residential community into which I was born and the place where I live and to which I am unconditionally committed. It has been a place where children in need of substitute care have been welcomed since 1899, and well over 1,000 children have lived here over the years. This is not the place to describe the particular and rather unusual nature of Mill Grove. But suffice it to say that it has been registered as a children's home for sixty years or more.

One of the undeniable and consistent features of the experiences of many, though not all, of the children is that for them Mill Grove functioned as a secure base. Many would say and have said that it has been their one secure base in life. As I write this, two young people have returned in the last couple of weeks: one after ten years trying to make his own way in life, the other after a year studying abroad as part of a degree. Both of them have been telling me how they have been accepted back unconditionally, and respected. They see us as reliable and resourceful friends. Demonstrably, they have used the place as a base for exploration, and are able to return, not as part of a defensive regression or out of dependency, but because they have chosen to do so, knowing that in time they will recommence their encounters with the outside world of learning, work and relationships.

Our conversations revealed the extent of our personal bonding and attachment, which contrast with their relatively poor and unpredictable attachments to their surviving parents.

Conclusion and coda

The work of John Bowlby has opened up new ways of seeing and understanding child development and mental health. Those of us who welcome and seek to implement it find it stands the test of time. One of the effects of the work has been to draw child care policy away from residential care which is seen as breaking the attachments and bonds between parents and children, towards family support and, where necessary, adoption and foster care. I maintain that Bowlby's work should be studied more carefully and the nature of residential care considered more objectively, not least the views of the children and young people past and present.

In North Wales there is a magnificent escarpment of rock running north to south along the eastern ridge of Cadair Idris, a mountain which for a long time was thought to be higher than Snowdon. I think it is part of a rift valley running through to Bala. Apart from lichen and moss little grows on its rocky outcrops that is visible to the naked eye, except a rowan tree – a mountain ash. For the past twenty years I have observed this tree's growth and resilience. It has found an unlikely perch in which to make its home, and put down its roots.

It has occurred to me that if this tree were a child or young person, some kindly social worker would have spotted its plight, done a risk assessment, and removed it, placing it in a friendlier environment. In the process the tree might have been killed or blighted of course. The risks to a child are similar.

What does this tree and Cadair Idris represent? The practical reality that some children will find a secure base in what others consider to be the most un-likely of places. These places may be a biological home, foster care, a local community, a school, or a residential establishment. Let us be careful before we undertake to remove them, albeit in what we conceive to be their best interests, and if we do, let us not immediately invoke the work of John Bowlby lest he repeats his view about an 'appalling misjudgement'.

References

Bowlby, E J M (1952) *Maternal Care and Mental Health: a report prepared on behalf of the World Health Organization as a contribution to the United Nations programme for the welfare of homeless children* Monograph Series No 2 Geneva, World Health Organization Second edition.

Bowlby, E J M (1953) *Child Care and the Growth of Love: Based by permission of the World Health Organization on the report Maternal Care and Mental Health* Abridged and edited by Margery Fry London, Penguin,

Bowlby, J (1988) *A Secure Base: clinical applications of attachment theory* London, Routledge

Kuhn, T S (1962) *The Structure of Scientific Revolutions* London, University of Chicago Press

Milligan, I (2006) Can we talk sense about fostering? www.childrenwebmag.com Issue 064 April

White, K J (2002) The ideology of residential care and fostering. In White, K J, ed, *Re-Framing Children's Services*, p231-242 London, NCVCCO

4

The contribution of the UK to child care policy, practice and research

Roger Bullock

Many developments in UK child care mirror those found in countries around the world and as such can be considered as part of the globalisation of public services. Policies to increase the amount of foster care, strengthen children's rights, provide for a growing number of children from abusive backgrounds, address difficulties of recruiting and retaining staff, controlling escalating costs and using independent agencies are almost universal. In this chapter, I identify some features of UK child care policy, practice and research that are unusual and where the contribution has been of international significance. This can help us understand not only how and why services have developed in different ways at different times in different places but suggest lessons that might be learned from international comparisons.

The United Kingdom comprises four countries each with its own legislation and tradition regarding provision for children living away from home. England, the largest country (population 50 million), shows similarities with Wales (population 3 million) and Northern Ireland (population 1.6 million) but Scotland (population 5 million) is noticeably different. This urges caution when generalising about child care in the United Kingdom.

The historical legacy

The arrangements for the care of separated children in the United Kingdom can only be fully understood in the context of the historical changes affecting each country. Most children separated for welfare reasons are now accommodated by foster families and many who would have been taken in to care in the past, such as young offenders, truants and children from poor families, now remain at home or are supported in the community. As in most economically developed countries, fostering is the preferred mode of care for those who need to be separated and the amount of residential provision for such children has declined in recent years. However, residential care is still significant for some groups; for example, in the UK it shelters 30 per cent of adolescents in care over the age of 15 and prison custody is increasingly used for teenage offenders.

The wider historical context illustrates several features of UK child care that are unusual, although not necessarily unique. For example, the history of residential homes and schools is marked by a close link with extremes of wealth and poverty (Parker, 1988). In England especially, the upper social classes have long sent their children to prestigious boarding schools called public schools, whose development was bound up with the growth of empire and religious division. This close link between residential schools and the top echelons in society is almost unique in the world.

The effect of this relationship was to produce not only a strong connection between residential education and social stratification but also a situation in which many top administrators and politicians were favourably disposed to residential solutions to social problems. The need to develop provision for deprived children has always been pressing. As far back as five hundred years ago the Poor Law, which governed provision for destitute and abandoned children following the dissolution of the Roman Catholic monasteries, was introduced.

These two strands in residential care and education have been especially important in England, Wales and Ireland but less so in Scotland and some parts of central Wales where the influential historical and economic factors are different. In Scotland, for instance, there was no mandatory poor rate and guardians did not have powers to borrow capital without gaining the consent of the ratepayers, who were usually disinclined to agree. Thus, there was relatively little workhouse building and there were few workhouse schools. Outdoor relief was also banned at various times, posing difficulties for the care of needy children. Complementing this situation was an extensive rural economy based on self-sufficiency where children were generally welcomed as extra hands and the boarding out payments as extra income. Thus, there was always more use of foster than residential care.

In addition to the tradition of elite residential schooling for the children of the wealthy, a distinctive feature of educational provision in the UK was the establishment in the 1930s and 1940s of a small set of self-styled 'progressive residential establishments'. These were founded by pioneers, such as Lyward and Neill, to help children with learning and behavioural difficulties (Bridgeland, 1971). Their approach was fashioned to contrast with the traditional public school and attracted interest and sponsorship from many *avant-garde* intellectuals of the time. Their message was highly relevant to child care thinking, not just in residential education and schools, but by its child-centred approach, its tolerance and acceptance of individuality and its co-education and lack of hierarchy in the staff and pupil worlds. Such schools exist world-wide but in the UK they have formed a more cohesive tranche of provision than elsewhere. As a result, there are groups of self-styled progressive boarding schools, therapeutic communities and schools for children with special educational needs, each with well established traditions and clear statements of purpose and function.

Similar developments occurred with regard to foster care. The UK now fosters as a matter of course children once deemed 'unfosterable', such as those who are behaviourally disordered, traumatised and disabled (Sinclair, 2005). Arrangements once thought impossible, such as placement with single parents or gay and lesbian carers are increasingly common and relationships for contact between the foster and the child's birth family are ever more varied. These developments have been encouraged by a legislative framework (the Children Act 1989) that focuses first on the needs of children and then on service responses to meet them, so encouraging the establishment of a wide range of preventative and specialist provision along a spectrum. Although the proportion of children in care placed in foster care has increased in the UK over the past 30 years, the number of children fostered at any one time has remained static because of an overall fall in the total number of children in care. So these new policies have necessitated the recruitment of different types of carers rather than more of the same.

The UK contribution to child care policy

Because the UK has a centralised child care system with most facilities provided or commissioned by the central Government, it has been easier to devise an overall strategy to care for children who need to live away from home. Hence, there have been continual discussions not only about the merits or otherwise of different care settings but also about the relationship between them. Change in one area has led to changes in others. For example, disenchantment with residential care in the 1960s following concerns about the institutionalisation of residents, abuse scandals, rising costs and staffing difficulties led to consideration of foster care as an alternative. (Although this perspective provided an intellectual impetus for reform, the reality is that foster care did not provide such an alternative, as most children who would have been placed residentially stayed at home.) Similarly, the success of foster care then influenced residential provision by stimulating policies that eventually abolished residential nursery provision and reduced the size of the homes that survived to make them less institutional.

Again, historical factors specific to the UK are important. The evacuation in the Second World War of over one million children from cities and vulnerable coastal towns to safe areas showed that fostering on a large scale was possible, although there was obviously an element of obligation in war time. The recommendations of a contemporary inquiry set up by the Government (the Curtis Committee, 1946) to look among other things at arrangements for the care of separated children further boosted this thinking by its major indictment of residential care in both the public and voluntary sectors.

This shift away from residential care coupled with a positive commitment to foster care from the 1950s onwards, supported by an argument that what was best for children was also the cheapest, is an almost unique combination in social policy. This situation was supported by the prevailing legislation (Children Act 1948) which made it a requirement that foster care should be used unless there was a good reason for not doing so. Another force, unusual at that time, was the training of specialist staff as recommended by the Curtis Committee to undertake this work. These workers were entitled 'boarding out officers'; with the terms 'child care officer' and 'child and family social worker' coming later. This professional structure contrasts with many approaches found in continental Europe, where pedagogic or therapeutic models are more common.

The break-up of the Poor Law and the creation of separate freestanding Children's Departments in each local authority in 1948 broke the dominance of residential provision in the public and voluntary sectors and led to the perception of services as a continuum of provision from which selections could be made to meet children's needs. In addition, the number of children in the care of voluntary organisations declined after the Second World War and so the impact of public policy was that much greater than before. Also significant was the fact that these post-war changes brought women into senior positions in local government and they were more overtly committed than their male counterparts had been to more 'home-like' provision, especially for girls.

In all these ways, the political, social and economic position of the United Kingdom after the Second World War – as a consequence of the war itself and the demographic changes occurring in society – was probably different from other countries, especially those where there had been foreign occupation, where there was a much larger voluntary (religious) sector wedded to institutions and, in federal states, like the US, where national policy was harder to apply. However, there were also significant differences between England and Wales and Scotland. In Scotland, 60 per cent of children in care were already boarded out by 1945 and there was a much smaller voluntary sector, mainly because of different Poor Law legislation and practice going well back into the nineteenth century and the opportunities for foster care offered by the highlands and islands system of crofters and cotters.

Thus, one might regard the UK as giving an international lead in child care following the Second World War, (and indeed before the 1914-18 War), although significant developments elsewhere, for example in Australia and Scandinavia, cannot be ignored. Furthermore, there was the perennial question of the quality of foster care and a need for continuing official scrutiny following revelations of poor standards, ill-treatment and high rates of breakdown. Coupled with this was an abiding, if undercurrent, concern in some local authorities, particularly the old industrial areas dominated by traditional left wing politics, with the principle of 'less eligibility', that is that those receiving care should not be better off as a result of receiving services funded from public money. This manifested itself in many ways, not least in a reluctance to pay foster parents any element of 'reward'.

Although official government policy encouraged foster care in the late 1940s, little systematic attention was paid to, for example, the training of foster parents or to how to recruit and retain them, unlike in Scandinavia. Indeed, there seemed to be little realisation of the impact that the increasing rate of women's employment would have upon the prospects of its expansion, so it remained a rather 'make do and mend' service. Yet, it is significant that when the central Government looked for simple ways of evaluating the effectiveness of different local authorities, fostering rates became something of a league table, with inspectors encouraged to press the poor performers to raise their game.

The UK's contribution to practice

It is more difficult to pin down the UK contribution to child care practice because of the extent of local variation and variations within local authorities. However, the growth of training (in the first instance geared to the development of foster care) previously mentioned was important. There was also a general, but largely unsubstantiated, view that after 1970 with the disappearance of Children's Departments (which were incorporated into larger Social Services Departments), the emphasis on foster care became diluted, especially with the incorporation of the old reform schools into the new system and the so-called loss of specialist child care skills. Certainly, professionals' case-loads became more mixed, at least for a while. Yet, historical research evidence showed that those areas with high and low rates of fostering had displayed these patterns for long periods, suggesting continuities of practice, traditions and opportunities. The latter probably had something to do with the fact that foster care (unlike adoption) had been traditionally a working-class institution.

Practice, however, was partly determined by regulation in the public sector. The first regulations for foster care were issued in 1889 and continued virtually unchanged for a hundred years. Amongst other things, these specified the terms on which foster parents were to take children, such as to bring them up as if they were their own. In addition, the frequency of visits by childcare staff was set, as were arrangements for medical examinations. Today, new and more exact standards are in place; nevertheless, the early regulations set certain requirements – albeit minimal – in practice. In many other countries where services are more disparate, standards are more likely to be set by the professional associations to which staff belong, but the UK Government has always seen a need to take on this responsibility, perhaps reflecting the lower qualifications of many child care staff in the UK.

The importance for practice of the organisation of the child care professions in the UK should not be overlooked. The Association of Children's Officers was set up in 1948 and became influential, running conferences and the like, and early on published its own Newsletter. With the establishment of BAAF – now British Agencies for Adoption and Fostering but originally solely concerned with adoption – and of the National Children's Bureau, a fragile network was established for the dissemination of ideas and practices about how best to develop services. These may not have been channels for the dissemination of research findings but there was a concern to promote best practice, as it was understood. And for many years there was not much research to be reported.

In terms of encouragement of best practice, the role of the Government inspectorate should not be forgotten. Indeed, the old Home Office Child Care Inspectorate was impressive, although it weakened after 1970 when Children's Departments became part of a larger organisation. Unlike now, many of its early reports were not published, although they were circulated within official (both central and local) circles and so had some influence. Many of these documents still read perceptively today.

The UK contribution to child care research

The UK has been a major contributor to research into separated children. The history of this work is interesting in itself. Serious research into residential care began in the 1940s with psychological studies into the effects of wartime separation, then came a concern with institutionalisation, followed in the 1960s by a tranche of more sophisticated studies to assess the effects of residential care, especially on delinquency. Subsequent work in the 1980s tended to take a different view and look at the role of residential care in wider child care services and while this usefully showed how children could become casualties of the system, it did rather turn attention away from outcomes, a situation not remedied until studies undertaken in the late 1990s (Clough *et al*, 2006).

Research into foster care has a shorter history. Not until the 1960s, and then only slowly, did research into foster care begin to take off. This was true internationally, although a few empirical studies had been undertaken in the US. But in foster care more than in residential care, what passed for research was often descriptive rather than explanatory, and often comprised little more than a catalogue of illustrative case-studies. Part of the problem was financial, the Social Science Research Council was not established until the 1960s, and there was a lack of interest in the area by researchers. What is surprising is how long it took the Government, (first the Home Office and later the Department of Health), to support and encourage research. This probably reflected a notion of how good practice was obtained, namely with individuals through sensitive and sympathetic insights. Even counting seemed to be a quite inappropriate approach and the first official statistics on children in care did not appear until 1952, and they were only rudimentary.

Since the 1980s, however, the amount of research into foster care has come to equal or even exceed that of residential care and there are major reviews now available on all aspects of child care provision. Moreover they are based on a considerable body of UK research (Department of Health, 1998; Sinclair, 2005; Clough *et al*, 2006). This has been useful not just for the new findings but also for disaggregating the concepts of foster and residential care, for example by distinguishing between short-term and long-term provision, placement with relatives as opposed to strangers, and for controlling for factors such as the age and previous history of the child and his or her family composition.

It has also identified better the problems of providing substitute care and its likely limitations and begun tentatively to indicate 'what works' – although focusing less on what does not work. Nevertheless, robust evidence based on Randomised Controlled Trials and Quasi Experimental Designs is still rare and it has to be said that there are no scientifically validated services for separated children in the UK. In this, UK child care research is inferior to many studies of children's services undertaken in the US.

Finally, through considerable efforts by researchers and commissioning agencies, research results have begun to be more successfully disseminated. This has involved considerable innovation in methods of communication and the establishment of organisations designed specifically for this purpose. Research funders are more willing than ever to devote resources to dissemination. What is less clear, however, is how far what it has to say has been acted upon, and if not why not.

Conclusion

The UK, I believe, has been at the forefront of policy and practice developments in child care in the last two decades and more so in the development and application of research into provision for separated children. However, its contribution can be judged as leading rather than being unique, as many other countries have similar claims. Yet several pressing questions remain, not least what precisely determines policy and practice and the role of research in this process. At the moment, the impact of child care research upon policy is influenced by the considerable continuing official commitment to foster care, the lack of extensive good alternatives and the cost issue. For reasons like these, governments seem more susceptible to any positive messages but less ready to hear and act upon those which sound a cautionary or doubtful note.

In looking to the future, it is noticeable that in the past five years current political interests in the UK have moved away from a narrow focus on provision for separated children towards the establishment of a children's service for all children in need. The most recent legislation, the Children Act 2002, seeks to improve outcomes (as opposed to service outputs) for children and families and to ensure consistency of services. It seeks this by integrating social, education and health services under an education umbrella in the hope that this will reduce professional divisions and encourage professionals from different disciplines to work together more effectively.

This approach raises rather different questions from previous debates about the merits of different forms of substitute care. Discussions focus on two areas. The first is how to integrate diverse organisational structures, professions and services to work together and what this actually means. The second involves consideration of the concepts necessary to underpin the common assessment methods necessary for multi-agency work. These have been suggested as needs, outcome, thresholds, risk and protective factors and services (Axford *et al*, 2005).

These are radical innovations emanating from frustrations with traditional child and family social work. The new approach perceives foster and residential care as interventions to meet needs, so avoiding putting them in opposition to each other, seeing them as alternatives or, worse still, using one to prevent the other. It also concentrates on what carers actually do rather than the administrative labels under which they operate. It remains to be seen whether this new thinking will attract the same level of international attention as did the earlier reforms in the care of separated children.

The author wishes to thank Professor Roy Parker for assistance in the preparation of the paper.

References

Axford, N, Berry, V, Little, M and Morpeth, L, eds (2005) *Forty years of research, policy and practice in children's services: a festschrift for Roger Bullock* Chichester, Wiley

Bridgeland, M (1971) *Pioneer Work with Maladjusted Children: a study of the development of therapeutic education* London, Staples

Clough, R, Bullock, R and Ward, A (2006) *What works in residential child care: a review of research evidence and the practical considerations* London, National Children's Bureau

Curtis, M CBE (1946) *Report of the Care of Children Committee* Cmnd 6922 London, His Majesty's Stationery Office

Department of Health (1998) *Caring for children away from home: messages from research* Chichester, Wiley

Parker, R A (1988) Residential care for children In Sinclair, I, ed, *Residential Care: The Research Reviewed*, Volume 2: Literature surveys commissioned by the Independent Review of Residential Care chaired by Gillian Wagner OBE PhD, p57-124 London, Her Majesty's Stationery Office

Sinclair, I (2005) *Fostering now: messages from research* London, Jessica Kingsley

5

Structural dynamics in society and innovations in the German residential care system

Peter Hansbauer

eginning in the late 1970s and during the 1980s fundamental changes took place in West Germany's institutional care system (*Heimerzie-hung*) which went almost completely unnoticed by the public (Blan-dow, 1987, 1989; Wolf, 1995). Significant among them were the organisational and conceptual differentiation of residential care, a reduction in repressive forms of accommodation and the spread of new forms of residential accommodation (*stationäre Unterbringung*) throughout West Germany.

This chapter argues that previous changes in education policy and in the labour market led to the adoption of new forms of residential care. Through critical analysis of the development of German residential care since the 1970s it examines the altered patterns of interpretation and rules of appropriateness which emerged within youth services. The central thesis is that the sociopolitical changes which started in the 1960s initiated developments which consequently undermined the legitimacy of traditional patterns of practice in youth services and thus prepared the ground for an accelerated diversification of youth services in the 1980s and 1990s (Hansbauer, 1999b).

It must be emphasised that the German youth welfare system is split between assessment and service provision. The statutory responsibilities in the field of youth work and youth welfare services delegated to the local authorities at the level of the *Landkreise* (district) and bigger cities are carried out by the youth offices (*Jugendämter*). The locally administered youth offices[1], usually in cooperation with the parents or legal guardians, first define the problem, then decide on the type and extent of care provision, and finally control the course of the provision. The actual care and treatment of the minors is mainly carried out by independent, so-called *freie Träger* (voluntary organisations), which often have a Christian background. Pursuant to the *Subsidiarität-sprinzip* (subsidiarity principle, which gives precedence of the voluntary youth services) the statutory youth services must subsidise and further the voluntary sector and must refrain from activities of its own where the voluntary youth services can provide suitable functions. Usually there is more than one service provider competing to offer a specific kind of care. Accordingly, despite the appearance of a corporate structure, the service providers (voluntary organisations) and purchasers of services (statutory bodies) meet in what is effectively a market (Anheier and Seibel, 1990).

The existence of this semi-market system means that it is not self-evident that organisational or conceptual improvements in children and youth care provisions will succeed, even if they are based on solid professional grounds. As providers are free to make their own organisational decisions – in contrast to systems in which youth services are for the most part publicly administered – innovations cannot be carried through in a hierarchical manner. On the other hand, when service providers (voluntary organisations) develop innovations of their own, such as non-residential individual care for example, the purchasers (statutory bodies) must be convinced first that the innovation holds advantages for them. Thus, as with any market, the lasting success of an innovation depends on the purchasers – in this case, the statutory bodies' – acceptance and continued purchase of the new service.

This leads directly to the question: why are certain innovations distributed widely throughout many regions or even nation-wide, whereas other innovations fail to establish themselves or stick only at a region level? Does an innovation have to fulfil specific criteria or must certain social and societal conditions be met before it can permanently establish itself and be distributed on a national basis? Are professional categories considered as relevant selection criteria by youth office social workers when choosing a certain programme?

Theoretical framework

If one searches on the level of a middle range theory (Merton, 1968) for a theoretical framework in which to answer these questions, an interesting starting-point can be found in Giddens' Theory of Structuration. Giddens (1984) defines social structure as both the medium and the outcome of social action. In other words, social structures are produced by action and are continually being reproduced through action. At the same time structures supply the raw materials (in the form of rules and resources) needed for action. According to Giddens, 'Action is a continuous process, a flow, in which the reflexive monitoring which the individual maintains is fundamental to the control of the body that actors ordinarily sustain throughout their day-to-day lives' (Giddens, 1984, p9).

That means Giddens bases his theoretical assumptions on actors capable of reflexive control and able to develop a theoretical understanding of both their own actions and those of others. They thus possess the ability to understand what they do while they are doing it, without of course knowing whether or not they will actually achieve their goal. The consequences of action are not exactly calculable, nor is it necessary that the conditions of action are completely understood by the actor. Rather, actors make decisions on the basis that they believe or know that certain actions give rise to certain effects. Thus the individually or collectively produced consequences of the action at a point in time X create the conditions for action at a later point in time Y, and so on.

What gives intentional action a certain direction or goal? In sociology it has long been acknowledged that people develop shared patterns of interpretation and accept norms and values through socialisation, which they follow more or less consciously. People often act according to social expectations which they believe are shared inter-subjectively and, by doing so, simultaneously reproduce these expectations within a certain social system or situation. Here the term 'expectation' stresses the fact that despite these collective shared patterns actors are also free to act in a way that deviates from what is expected.

Decision-making theory occasionally uses the concept 'rules of appropriateness', when talking about these inter-subjectively shared expectations (March and Olsen, 1989). This means that others' expectations of what actions are appropriate in a certain situation influence the agents' actions because the agent anticipates that these expectations exist. Apart from rituals, though, the criterion of appropriateness is vague in relation to concrete actions. The expectation of appropriate behaviour therefore constitutes a type of corridor within which relevant problems arise and corresponding solutions are developed (Ortmann, 1995).

Expectations of how to behave appropriately within a certain social system or situation involve collectively shared interpretation schemes, which lend them legitimacy and give them a social meaning. Organisational theory describes this pattern of shared interpretation using a range of terms such as culture (Wildavsky, 1987), ideology (Brunsson, 1982), theory-in-use (Argyris, 1985), or cognitive map (Weick and Bougeon, 1986). However, if the coherence and clarity of this shared pattern of interpretation is lost, the tendency towards rule-following dwindles as well. Action then begins to show increasingly anomic features and decision making becomes more and more contingent (March, 1994).

Where situations are less structured by collectively shared interpretation schemes, it is more likely that reflexive interests will guide actions. Reflexive interests may be defined as those which are not directly focused on the achievement of a certain state or event but instead focus on the conditions which allow the realisation of such interests in the first place. Interests can be seen as reflexive when, for example, they are focused on expanding the scope of one's own interest realisation, on achieving dominance in a certain sphere of interest by monopolising authorisation, or on increasing the control over one's own interest realisation and raising one's own decision autonomy (Schimank, 1995).

The German residential care system to the end of the home campaigns in the 1960s

After the Second World War, residential care was mostly conducted in reformatories. Even though there were ambitious efforts to promote family-like care settings – eg the Munich Orphanage (Mehringer, 1976) – the actual occurrence of this type of care setting was rather marginal. Gertraude Schulz wrote in the *Handbook of Residential Care*,

> The family-like structured home with about 25 children, demanded by experts, is relatively rare. Usually the existing homes are a good deal bigger, since the setup and maintaining of small units is too expensive [...] for historic reasons most homes were of medium or big size. In the south of Germany smaller homes were established, while in the north and west the homes are normally bigger. The amount of inmates in the south of Germany reaches up to 100 children; while in the north quite often a couple of hundred children are living in one home. (Schultz, 1966, p285)

The institutional character of youth welfare which predominantly – albeit not exclusively – distinguished residential care up into the 1970s was typified by the fact that it viewed its clientele not as personal beings but as cases. Lacking personal identities, clients were seen as bearers of symptoms which had to be altered to meet the demands of a societal blueprint of normality (Niederberger, 1997, p135). It was this perceptual transformation which allowed the degree of standardised daily life typical of these institutions (eg Wenzel, 1973; Colla, 1973). If, however, residential care concentrates too categorically upon conformity and social discipline – as was the case historically – the socio-educational provision organisations find themselves in a structural dilemma: 'If the deviant behaviour becomes the single goal of normalising inter-vention, the frequent consequence is an immediate breach of confidence in the relationship' (Japp, 1986 p89). The goal of normalisation is thus threatened by the organisation's complete focus upon the symptoms.

Up until the 1990s residential care reacted to this dilemma in one of two ways. The first strategy was to systematically attribute the unintended effects of a repressively and minutely organised youth care to the client (also Wolffers-dorff, 1993, p59). This led to a range of responses: (superficial) adaptation to the inner-institutional system of rules on the part of the minors until their discharge from the institution; escape from the institution; or the transfer of rebellious minors to another institution where repressive elements were more strongly pronounced (Wenzel, 1970, p145; Freigang, 1986). If these minors continued to behave inappropriately, they were placed in closed institutes, which amounted to prison-like internment. However, this created a problem: holding the clientele solely responsible for institutional problems at least partially conflicted with the normalisation goal, and this could not be maintained without simultaneously damaging the legitimacy of the entire residential care system.

A second strategy was therefore tried within the institutions. This involved the partial separation of formal structures and informal practices in order to soften the effects of repressive rules and regulations (Goffman, 1968). Against the backdrop of a hierarchical-authoritarian formal structure and clearly de-fined reformatory goals (the inculcation of the work ethic as well as confine-ment and reform), direct dealings between clients and counsellors involved secret trades and compensations – 'If I give you this or that privilege, you will go to bed tonight on time without causing me any trouble' etc. These informal practices prevented problems of a structural nature between the two groups from escalating beyond control. In this way the goal of normalisation could be justified externally without having to radically impose it internally.

The systematic separation of formal structures and informal practices re-quired, however, that what actually went on within the institutions remained hidden from the outside world. Such a strategy was therefore linked to certain technical and spatial conditions, eg control over the client's communication with the outside world (visitor surveillance, limited telephone access, mail inspection, etc) or the geographical isolation of the institutions (Freigang and Wolf, 2001, p39).

It also required that the service purchasers – the youth offices – were generally satisfied with reports about the clients from institutional staff, and moreover that they did not probe further. Only in this way could it be guaranteed that the management of institutional care was spared from further scrutiny. As a consequence, this lack of transparency allowed both the separation of structures and practices and the continuing systematic blaming of clients for their failed resocialisation.

This decade-long and relatively stable situation was severely disrupted for the first time by the so-called *Heimkampagnen* (home campaigns), youth revolts in residential care homes during the late 1960s. With the support of students, professors and a critical press, the residential care system was, for a brief period, made visible to the public eye (Almstedt and Munkwitz, 1982, p29; Schrapper, 1990; Arbeitsgruppe Heimreform, 2000, p126) and the first reforms were set in motion. Although the immediate impact of the home campaigns was quantitatively rather modest, a number of innovative projects did arise and, in certain cases, led to home reforms (Blandow, 1989, p283). The momentum it created for reform is not to be underestimated: the short-term alliance of politicised youth, critical students, professors and the press led to public realisation of the dilemma described above. The young people themselves, as obstinate and suppressed personalities, were thus suddenly of significance. Consequently statutory bodies and voluntary organisations had to recognise their clients as people, not just bundles of problems, and so the legitimising factors necessary to support the two strategies described above began to crumble. In order to explain why this was so momentous, it is necessary for the working conditions particular to youth services to be briefly outlined.

More so than in other areas of society, social work, especially youth services, offers its employees potentially satisfying work in many ways: by building primary relationships, by the possible identification with others and by dealing with personal problems (Wolf, 1999). The occupation's emphasis lies in the interaction between people instead of between people and things (Hasenfeld, 1983, p114). However, while this can be seen to make professional youth service workers comparable to doctors or lawyers, who also possess much flexibility during daily work and can be characterised by a high degree of occupational identification (Plake, 1978, p294), youth service professionals do not possess a body of standard knowledge in a similar way to these professions.

This, as emphasised above, is due to the fact that residential care deals with social objects about which neither initiating factors nor empirical effects can be clearly reconciled through a causal connection (Brim and Wheeler, 1966). Because of this 'technological deficit' (Luhmann and Schorr, 1982), the professional methodology of problem-solving strategies, the standard knowledge needed to achieve goals is relatively limited (Glisson, 1992). This high degree of intrinsic motivation on the one hand and the absence of technologically based standard knowledge on the other inevitably increase the susceptibility of professional youth work to changes in socially dominant patterns of legitimacy and interpretation precisely because pedagogical action must predominantly be derived from normative orientations.

The alteration of societal conditions in residential care following 1970

Reforms are always carried out within an historic-social context which, as an external social condition, influences agents' actions. Therefore, in order to understand the far-reaching upheavals within institutional care, which for the most part could first be observed during the 1980s – more than ten years after the home campaigns – it is necessary to examine the alteration of societal conditions during the 1970s more closely. Only then does the enormous impetus of the *Heimkritik* (criticism of homes) and the tremendous decline of legitimacy become clear.

During the mid-1960s the backward post-war politico-educational atmosphere, characterised by its yearning for peace and quiet, gave way to the consciousness that the economic upturn also had to correspond to an intellectual upturn, that the world was changing at a speed which demanded a response from the educational system (Becker, 1983, p332). This turn-about initiated the renunciation of a need-oriented education policy, which was officially acknowledged by the German education council's (*Bildungsrat*) structural plan in 1970. This legitimated the educational expansion, at that time in full swing, independent of the employment systems development (Becker, 1983, p333). Parallel to this, the consolidation of the university system, as recommended by the scientific council (*Wissenschaftsrat*), had been taking place since the 1960s.

The consequent relative shift of the pupil population away from the *Hauptschule (*basic secondary schools) to the more advanced Realschulen (secondary modern schools) and Gymnasien (grammar schools), as well as the rapid expansion of relevant courses of study at universities, led to increased social work and social science graduates on the labour market. This process was reinforced by the large number of births during the baby-boom years (Korte, 1983). This increase in academically qualified personnel could, for the most part, be absorbed by an enormous expansion in employment possibilities. Between 1970 and 1987 alone the number of people employed in social work occupations increased from around 150,000 to 400,000 (Rauschenbach, 1990, p276; Schilling, 2001).

This expansion of employment, however, led to a weakening of existing shared interpretation schemes and potentially the stability of traditional approaches to residential care (Hansbauer, 1996). As new employees have to be socialised within a social context, a dramatic change of personnel in a setting increases the risk that existing everyday routines lose their self-evident nature. The enormous employment increase by itself, therefore, most likely led to the gradual decrease in the commitment to collectively shared orientations.

During the 1980s there was at the same time a surplus of qualified employees on the West German labour market (Leenen, 1992). Despite the ever-increasing employment rate, the number of unemployed persons in the field of social occupations continued to grow, stabilising at a level of about 50,000. Employment policy reacted to this development by initiating a rapid expansion of government-funded Job Creation Schemes between 1983 and 1987; in 1984, for instance, there was an increase from 9,000 to 20,000 in the number of social work employees in Job Creation Schemes (Leenen, 1992, p511). Integration in this government-funded sector of the labour market was only possible, though, if it could be proved that the new posts contributed to dealing with (new) social problems. This not only led to a growing appreciation of social problems; it also brought about an increase in the rate of innovation in the field of social work, all the more as the Job Creation Schemes heightened the possibility of continually developing new justifications for action (eg in the form of concepts).

Therefore, the 1970s and 1980s were a period of ground-breaking innovations not only in residential care but in the whole area of social work. During this period a great variety of care settings and socio-educational provision emerged, which shaped the organisational field of youth welfare and contiguous fields, such as socio-educational family help (*Sozialpädagogische Familienhilfe*), detached youth work (*Mobile Jugendarbeit*), work with youth subcultures (*Soziokulturelle Arbeit*), assistance for drug users and addicts (*Drogenhilfe*), special arrangements for girls (*Mädchenarbeit*), streetwork, centres for child protection (*Kinderschutzzentren*), centres for physically abused women (*Frauenhäuser*) and much more (Müller, 2001). In many cases these provisions emerged in the context of self-help and initiative groups, which means that they were also an organisational alternative to the established voluntary organisations.

The qualitative changes in the youth services personnel were likely to be as decisive as the increased number of employees. Starting in the 1970s, a continuing trend can be observed towards a higher qualification of youth services personnel (Rauschenbach *et al*, 1988; Rauschenbach and Schilling, 1997). This increasing professionalisation of youth services would have been almost unthinkable without the parallel expansion of the university system and the related development of social work as an academic discipline. It was in 1969 that certified courses of study for university-trained youth workers were first introduced, and since 1971 there had been the development of universities for applied science (*Fachhochschulen*) and the conversion of colleges (*Fachschulen*) for social work into universities for applied science (Rauschenbach, 1990, p249).

Many newly hired professors now had a personal interest – in terms of legitimisation and leaving their mark – in exploiting the possibilities for developing alternatives to existing services, and their professional status and involvement in innovative services gave further impetus to change. The extent to which they took up new developments already in practice, for instance, provided a renewed strengthening of the dynamics of development shown above.

The qualitative changes just outlined were decisive for residential care. They accelerated an alignment of practitioners' discourses with those active in the universities at that time, which were linked to new empirical results of youth research. A paradigmatic change was becoming more and more apparent in a shift from fixed to diverse conceptions of what is considered 'normal'. This change manifested itself, for instance, in a general change in service philosophy from seeking conformity to helping young people cope with life (Böhnisch and Schefold, 1985). Repressive forms of residential care were discredited and replaced by qualitatively different (negotiation-oriented) frames of reference for pedagogical action. This development was reinforced by staff now working in residential care who were more familiar with reflecting on daily practice and experienced in thinking through and developing new approaches.

The 1970s and 1980s were thus marked by considerable upheaval and restructuring in the labour market for social occupations. This consequently brought about new developments or considerably accelerated those already under way. Not all these developments were consistent and some provoked bitter conflicts. Nevertheless, together they led to the reform of the dominant form of youth welfare which had been astonishingly stable, despite widespread pressure, during the late 1970s.

Organisational and conceptual changes in residential accommodation

While within the West German youth services repressive forms of youth care fell into disrepute and lost legitimacy, the system of public welfare was confronted with severe consequences. Not least was the fact that the expectations of other societal systems working together with youth services such as the police, school and the media, did not change at the same speed, and this resulted in conflicts between the various organisations.

As indicated, the West German residential care system tended to move young people from one institution to another and finally, if nothing worked, confine them in 'closed' residential care (Wolffersdorff *et al*, 1996). This practice was significantly challenged by the changes described above, with closed residential care – the most extreme form of repressive care – abolished in several *Länder* (states) and greatly restricted in others during the 1980s. Metaphorically speaking, the nine-headed hydra's ugliest head was cut off, the one upon which the face of repression was most conspicuous. The natural end of the line was now missing, though the practice of shifting rebellious minors from one institution to another within the residential care system continued to be a problem.

We have seen that this led to problems, mainly on the system borders of residential care. Institutional problems arose in the child and youth services committees (*Jugendhilfeausschuss*), at that time called youth welfare committees, where, due to the two-tier system of the youth office, the expectations of the political system collided with those of youth services.[2] Conflict also developed where employees of the youth offices had direct contact with schools, press, neighbourhood residents or police officers and were under tremendous pressure to take young people into or back into the residential care system. In order to meet the pressure of expectation on the youth offices from the outside and a loss of public legitimacy, these youths had to be processed by the youth services.

Alternative forms of care were therefore needed which could be presented to other societal systems as a possible solution to 'the youth problem' while being simultaneously compatible with new, negotiation-oriented forms of youth care, based on more open ideas of normality which gradually began to predominate in the youth services. Alternatives, in the shape of established programmes, were not available at that point, so the youth offices were increasingly willing to consider innovations which held a solution for their problems. The type of solution involved was in many cases secondary.

These intersecting problems on the one hand and the parallel quantitative and qualitative changes concerning the employment structure in social work on the other hand were the main reasons for tremendous changes in the institutional care system. They provided a unique opportunity for alternative types of care, often non-residential and individual, to establish themselves permanently while at the same time the existing forms of residential care came under further pressure. If one looks at these developments in the late 1970s and 1980s in a more systematic way, two particular lines of development are quite obvious. First, there was an increase of placements in foster care and a growth of small organisational units in residential care and attempts to decentralise in greater ones respectively. Secondly, there was a conceptual differentiation of care settings, which had previously relatively homogeneous.

In the second half of the 1970s the amount of foster care placements and placements in small residential homes was rising quite remarkably (Blandow, 1987). This was partly due to the influence of the *Zwischenbericht der Kommission Heimerziehung* (Intermediate Report of the Commission for Residential Care) (1977), which argued in favour of a projected development of 'small organisational units' in residential care and for a placement policy with the intention of situating children as close as possible to their former home areas.

The report stimulated and legitimated processes which were already ongoing. At the same time the traditional homes increased their attempts to decentralise their organisations. They moved out small units and groups from the core institutions and settled them in a nearby residential neighbourhoods, to be as 'normal' as possible. Moreover, they increasingly tried to establish socio-educational provision in socially disadvantaged quarters or areas. In parallel, the traditional pattern of organising residential care for groups of minors became more and more flexible. The size and composition of groups began to vary, as did the number and qualifications of staff.

Since these new organisational arrangements were largely negotiated between single voluntary organisations and the locally administered youth offices or statutory bodies on the level of the states (*Länder*), which were the purchasers of socio-educational provision, these changes occurred rather disparately at different paces and with significant regional variations. As a result of this, at a nation-wide level the structure of service provision as well as the organisational framework of residential care became increasingly heterogeneous.

As mentioned, changes occurred not only on an organisational level but as well on a conceptual level. Conceptual changes simultaneously legitimated organisational changes and led to more heterogeneity too. Analytically speaking, at least five different rationales for a conceptual diversification and strategies of change can be identified, although in practice quite often a mixture of arguments can be found (Hansbauer, 1999a, p55).

1 *An expansion of socio-educational provision for children with specific problems*

These provisions were mostly focused on specific problems or a specific definition of problems by 'experts', to be 'cured' by a special kind of treatment or special group settings and trainings. In addition to an enhancement of therapeutic measures, certain target groups were to be encouraged by special social pedagogic methods and assistance. Examples of this approach were special arrangements for (disadvantaged) girls and young women, for ethnic minorities or vocational training activities and programmes for young persons with difficulties to get into labour market (Sander, 1988).

2 *An expansion of socio-educational provision for young persons and young adults who needed preparation for a 'normal' life after residential care*

Based on the argument that residential care creates exceptional circumstances whose normative and social structure differs quite remarkably from the outside world, the transfer from one system to the other creates enormous strain for the former residents. Beginning in the 1970s aftercare provision was established to ease that transition. This kind of provision can be arrayed along a continuum, beginning with special group settings to make the inmates more independent in the core institution (*Verselbständigungsgruppen*), groups that were outside the core institution (*Außenwohngruppen*) and accommodation with social worker support (*Betreutes Wohnen*) (Stephan, 1985).

3 *An expansion of socio-educational provision which is derived from pedagogical models or ideas of living together*

The rationale for this type of provision was based on – often idealised and ideological – ideas and visions of what can be achieved by residential care. Some of these models are inspired by ideas of a more egalitarian society and of a utopian character, like youth collectives (*Jugendwohnkollektive*); others followed more traditionalistic patterns, like groups that were organised similar to families (*familienanaloge Wohngruppen*). The promoters of these services often attributed characteristics like privacy, lucidity, stability and continuity of relations, commitment and positive interaction to the family, which were often more wishful thinking than what could be found in reality.

4 *An expansion of socio-educational individual care*

Beginning in the 1980s the first approaches emerged to dispense with the traditional model of the group, which had been the dominating organisational pattern in residential care for centuries (Späth, 1988, p25). The promoter's main argument for this new form of non-institutional individual care (*ambulante Einzelbetreuung*) was that it is seldom helpful to bring a young person with behavioural problems together with more young people with behavioural problems. Quite often, this leads to aggravation rather than to a reduction of behavioural problems. Instead, a young person who needs intensive support to achieve social integration should receive intensive socio-educational individual care depending on their needs. This could, for instance, mean not only living alone in an inner-city apartment with regular support provided by a social worker, together with emergency telephone back-up, but also living abroad for some time or engaged in some intense sporting activity, such as crossing the Alps together with a social worker.

5 *An expansion of socio-educational provision in day groups*

Although the first attempts to loosen the principle of twenty-four-hour care in residential education date back to the 1950s (Späth, 1989), it was not until the late 1970s that day groups became an independent kind of provision separate from residential care. These day groups are intended to support the development of the child or young person by social learning in the group, assistance with additional education and parental work so as to allow the child or young person to remain in his or her family.

Residential care in a reunited Germany

The first half of the 1990s was politically dominated by the aftermath of the fall of the Berlin Wall and the reunification of Germany. In the years following the reunification process the political aim was to establish a social infrastructure and youth welfare system in the area of former East Germany equivalent to that of former West Germany. During this time a lot of voluntary organisations from the western parts of the country built up new branches or adopted new established voluntary organisations in the eastern parts, while at the same time the educational and university system was aligned to western standards often with staff from the former West Germany.

Moreover, large numbers of the staff in the youth welfare system of the former East Germany undertook further training as social workers according to the western model or were put onto additional training schemes. This enormous transfer of staff, concepts, knowledge and organisational structures on the one hand enabled a rapid adjustment of the youth welfare system in the so-called *neue Länder* (new states) to western standards, but on the other hand prevented indigenous development in the former East Germany.

In 1990/91 a new law for child and youth services in Germany came into effect. The Child and Youth Services Act (Social Code Book VIII) was the outcome of a discussion by experts (ministries, professional organisations, umbrella organisations etc) which lasted for more than twenty years in the former West Germany and coincided with the reunification process. The new law legitimated the changes in service provision already accomplished and compelled other voluntary organisations which had not adapted to new structures yet to do so. Following the rather dynamic changes in the 1980s and the expansion into the former East Germany, a tendency to consolidate was quite obvious in the field of voluntary organisations, but the momentum for innovative change, however, then shifted from there to the youth offices and statutory bodies.

For the youth offices – the service purchasers – the new law entailed three important changes which led to considerable alterations in organisational structures and internal procedures. First, the new law imposed the actual costs of socio-educational provision for children with problems completely on the local authorities at the level of districts (*Landkreis*) and bigger cities. (Previously, these costs were partly defrayed by the *Länder*.) Secondly, the new law obliged the youth offices to develop a so-called 'help plan' (§ 36 Social Code Book VIII).

Sentence two of paragraph 36 is especially worth noting,

> If there is reason to presume that socio-educational provision will have to be granted for an extended period of time, the decision about the kind of provision indicated in the individual case shall be taken by way of co-operation among several

qualified staff. They shall together with the person who has the right of care and custody and the child or young person set up a help plan as a basis for organising the specific provision. Such plan shall state the educational requirements, the type of provision to be granted and the necessary benefits. Such qualified staff shall regularly review the chosen type of provision for continued suitability and need. If other persons, services or establishments are involved in the provision of help such persons, services or establishments or their employees shall participate in setting up and reviewing the help plan.

Thirdly, the new law allocated the statutory youth services the overall responsibility to organise an adequate service infrastructure and basic provision in every district or bigger city. Recognised voluntary youth service organisations were allowed to participate early in all stages of these planning activities (Youth services planning, § 80 Social Code Book VIII).

These last two legal changes in particular ended the long-lasting practice of written reports by institutional staff about clients in residential care and required the social workers in the youth offices to see their clients regularly and review the provision of services. Before, it was quite common that social workers in the youth offices rarely met their clients or the staff of the organisations where they were placed. This, and the need for the systematic planning of services, increased the transparency for statutory bodies of what was really going on in residential care. On the other hand the Child and Youth Services Act stimulated cooperation between youth offices and voluntary youth service organisations and prepared the ground for community-based (*sozialräumliche*) and integrated youth welfare services.

In addition to legal changes, the statutory bodies' growing financial crisis – due to demographic and social shifts, growing unemployment and periodic payments to the *neue Länder* – forced many local authorities to rethink and reorganise their internal structures. Although not always successful, the predominant objective was to reduce the cost of child and youth welfare. This could be achieved either by a rise in productivity in service provision or by a cutback of services. Both strategies were applied during the following years. These approaches were ideologically flanked by a rapid change in the dominant welfare state model in Germany, which had been based on the idea of a maximisation of general welfare since the 1960s. In the 1980s, and particulary in the 1990s, this welfare state model was more and more displaced by ideas of private markets and a competition-based service provision (Naschold, 1993, p17).

It was unavoidable that changes in the statutory sector entailed consequences for the voluntary organisations which were largely dependent on public means. Whether they wanted it or not, voluntary organisations were affected by the new public management approaches tried out by a growing number of local authorities. Core elements of these new approaches were, amongst others, the design and development of standards for service performance and output, the application of new management tools for cost and service control and a tendency to a more cost-conscious competition (Reichard, 1994). Increasing competition and the need for better and more effective service documentation encouraged voluntary organisations to optimise and professionalise their internal management skills.

These developments were furthered by the amendment of the Social Code Book VIII at the end of the 1990s which required youth offices and voluntary organisations to make joint agreements on benefits and services, charges and quality improvement (§ 78a *et sgg* Social Code Book VIII). As mentioned above, according to the Social Code Book VIII the youth offices in Germany are not only paying for socio-educational provision, they are also fairly independent in designing their organisational structures and creating their local youth welfare policies. Therefore these developments led to an increasing regional disparity – depending on the financial capacities of the local authorities – and to a growing heterogeneity in service provision on a nationwide level.

However, it was not only changes on a legal and administrative level that led to more flexibility and to further diversification of services; new professional approaches did as well. Especially in the second half of the 1990s, new approaches promoting community-based service provision became increasingly prominent. Most notably the Eighth Child and Youth report (*8. Kinder- und Jugendbericht*), which was published in 1990 by a group of experts on behalf of the Government, promoted the so-called 'wrapped-around approach' (*Lebensweltorientierung*) in child and youth welfare.

The general idea behind it was that child and youth welfare should be more oriented to the everyday lives of clients. The approach aimed at a normalisation of child and youth welfare and the repeal of repressive functions. People should draw on child and youth services whenever they are in need for it, as they draw on other local services. The report states, 'Regional service provision means the linkage of child and youth welfare to quasi-naturally grown, palpably local and regional structures as well as the development of sustainable regional and local social networks' (*Bundesministerium für Familie, Seniorem, Frauen und Jugend*, 1990, p17). Therefore the Eighth Child and Youth report stipulated the principle of regional service provision, which during the following years provided a legitimate basis too, for more regional and community based service provision and further diversification of services.

Professional as well as monetary motives therefore stimulated a number of pilot projects in various towns and districts in Germany, which quite often relate to each other. On the level of ideal types, one group of projects – rooted in the tradition of community work – attempted to encourage the inter-linkage of youth welfare and existing local networks. Differing in practice – although related to the same objective – these numerous approaches tried to organise child and youth welfare services completely on a local basis (Hinte and Treeß, 2006). The other group of projects focused more on the relation-ship of statutory bodies and voluntary organisations (Peters and Koch, 2004). One joint element of these approaches is to strengthen the overall respon-sibility of the voluntary organisations for certain local areas (*Sozialraum*) by improving the cooperation between youth offices and voluntary organisa-tions and greater involvement of voluntary organisations in processes of decision-making about the type and extent of socio-educational provision for children with problems. That way socio-educational provision becomes more flexible and better adjusted to individual requirements of clients.

Looking from that point into the future, it seems highly likely that the 'entropy' in Germany's institutional care system will rise. We will be con-fronted with a growing regional disparity in service provision, depending both on local policies and the financial power of certain regions and cities. It is not necessary to be a clairvoyant to predict that the service infrastructure of child and youth welfare will be much more disparate in the near future than today and that we will find a far greater diversity – from a professional point of view – of 'good' and 'bad' socio-educational provision for minors with problems. Therefore, one of the biggest challenges for the future of child and youth services will be to prevent the lowering of standards for basic service provision, especially in less wealthy areas. It is not acceptable that the region where a child accidentally lives should have such enormous influence on the allocation of public support and chances in live.

Notes

1 Currently more than 600 youth offices exist in Germany. Since the *Social Code Book VIII*, which is the legal basis for the German child and youth services, is only a framework law, the local policies concerning childhood and youth differ quite a lot.

2 The youth services committee usually consists of 15 voting members. According to the Child and Youth Services Act (Social Code Book VIII) three-fifths of the voting members must be members of the elected council of the statutory body or women and men with experience in youth work and youth welfare services elected by the council, with two fifths of the voting members being women

and men elected by the council on the nomination of recognised voluntary youth service organisations acting within the territory of the statutory body. The youth services committee can deal with all matters of youth work and youth welfare services, especially with discussions of current problems of young people and their families as well as suggestions and proposals for the development of youth work and youth welfare services, youth services planning, and funding of and public support for the voluntary sector. It has the right to pass resolutions on matters of youth work and youth welfare services within the limits of the funds supplied, statutes enacted and resolutions adopted by the council.

References

Almstedt, M and Munkwitz, B (1982) *Ortsbestimmung der Heimerziehung: Geschichte, Bestandsaufnahme, Entwicklungstendenzen* Weinheim; Basel, Beltz

Anheier, H K and Seibel, W, eds (1990) *The Third Sector. Comparative Studies of Nonprofit Organisations* Berlin, de Gruyter

Arbeitsgruppe Heimreform (2000) *Aus der Geschichte lernen: Analyse der Heimreform in Hessen* (1968-1983) Frankfurt/Main, Internationale Gesellschaft für erzieherische Hilfen

Argyris, C (1985) Interventions for improving leadership effectiveness *Journal of Management Development*, 4:30-50

Becker, H (1983) Bildungspolitik. In Benz, W, ed, *Die Bundesrepublik Deutschland: Geschichte in drei Banden Band 2: Gesellschaft*, p324-350 Frankfurt/Main, Fischer Taschenbuch Verlag

Blandow, J (1988) Heimerziehung in den 80er Jahren Materilien und Einschätzungen zur jüngeren Entwicklung der Heimerziehung. In Peters, F, ed, *Entwicklungsperspektiven in der Heimerziehung: Jenseits von Familie und Anstalt*, p28-49 Bielefeld, Böllert

Blandow, J (1989) Heimerziehung und Jugendwohngemeinschaften. In Blandow, J and Faltermeier, J, eds, *Erziehungshilfen in der Bundesrepublik Deutschland Stand und Entwicklungen*, p276-315 Stuttgart; Berlin; Köln; Mainz, Kohlhammer

Böhnisch, L and Schefold, W (1985) *Lebensbewältigung Soziale und pädagogische Verständigungen an den Grenzen der Wohlfahrtsgesellschaft* Weinheim, München, Juventa-Verlag

Brim, O G and Wheeler, S (1966) *Socialization after childhood: two essays* New York, Wiley

Brunsson, N (1982) The irrationality of action rationality: Decisions, ideologies and organizational action *Journal of Management Studies*, 19:29-44

Bundesministerium für Familie, Senioren, Frauen und Jugend, ed (1990) *Achter Jugendbericht Bericht über Bestrebungen und Leistungen der Jugendhilfe* Bonn, Bundesministerium für Familie, Senioren, Frauen und Jugend

Colla, H E (1973) *Der Fall Frank. Exemplarische Analyse der Praxis öffentlicher Erziehung* Neuwied; Berlin, Luchterhand

Forschungsgruppe Jugendhilfe Klein-Zimmern (1992) *Familiengruppen in der Heimerziehung Eine empirische Studie zur Entwicklung und Differenzierung von Betreuungsmodellen* Frankfurt/Main; Bern; New York; Paris, Lang

Freigang, W (1986) *Verlegen und Abschieben: Zur Erziehungspraxis in Heimen* Weinheim, München, Juventa-Verlag

Freigang, W and Wolf, K (2001) *Heimerziehungsprole: Sozialpädagogische Porträts* Weinheim; Basel, Beltz

Giddens, A (1984) *The Constitution of Society: introduction to the theory of structuration* Berkeley, University of California Press

Glisson, C (1992) Structure and technology in human service organizations. In Hasenfeld, Y, ed, *Human Services as Complex Organizations*, p3-23 Newbury Park, Sage

Goffman, E (1968) *Asylums: Essays on the Social Situation of Mental Patients and Other Inmates* Harmondsworth, Penguin

Hansbauer, P (1996) 'Mikrorationalitäten' im Verwaltungsalltag Dargestellt am Beispiel der 'Hilfen zur Arbeit' (§§18ff BSHG) in einer Sozialverwaltung *Soziale Welt*, 47:68-91

Hansbauer, P (1999a) *Traditionsbrüche in der Heimerziehung: Analysen zur Durchsetzung der ambulanten Einzelbetreuung* Münster, Votum

Hansbauer, P (1999b) Wie aus Innovationen Institutionen werden *Zeitschrift für Erziehungswissenschaft*, 2:73-97

Hasenfeld, Y (1983) *Human Service Organizations* Englewood Cliffs, Prentice Hall

Hinte, W and Treeß, H (2006) *Sozialraumorientierung in der Jugendhilfe: Theoretische Grundlagen, Handlungsprizipien und Praxisideen einer kooperativ-integrativen Pädagogik* Weinheim; München, Juventa-Verlag

Japp, K P (1986) *Wie psychosoziale Dienste organisiert werden Widersprüche und Auswege* Frankfurt/Main; New York, Campus-Verlag

Korte, H (1983) Bevölkerungsstruktur und Entwicklung. In Benz, W, ed, *Die Bundesrepublik Deutschland: Geschichte in drei Banden Band 2: Gesellschaft*, p13-34 Frankfurt/Main, Fischer Taschenbuch Verlag

Leenen, W R (1992) Der Arbeitsmarkt für Sozialarbeiter und Sozialpädagogen Ein kritischer Rückblick auf die 80er Jahre *Neue Praxis*, 22:503-523

Luhmann, N and Schorr, K E (1982) Das Technologiedefizit der Erziehung und die Pädagogik In Luhmann, N and Schorr, K E, eds, *Zwischen Technologie und Selbstreferenz*, p11-40 Frankfurt/Main, Suhrkamp

March, J G (1994) *A Primer on Decision Making: How Decisions Happen* New York, Free Press

March, J G and Olsen, J P (1989) *Rediscovering Institutions The Organizational Basis of Politics* New York, Free Press

Mehringer, A (1976) *Heimkinder: Gesammelte Aufsätze zur Geschichte und Gegenwart der Heimerziehung* München; Basel, E Reinhardt

Merton, R K (1963) *Social Theory and Social Structure* New York, Free Press, revised and enlarged edition

Müller, C W (2001) *Helfen und Erziehen: soziale Arbeit im 20 Jahrhundert* Weinheim; Basel, Beltz

Naschold, F (1993) *Modernisierung des Staates: zur Ordnungs- und Innovationspolitik des öffentlichen Sektors* Berlin, Ed Sigma

Niederberger, J M (1997) *Kinder in Heimen und Pflegefamilien: Fremdplazierung in Geschichte und Gesellschaft* Bielefeld, Kleine

Ortmann, G (1995) *Formen der Produktion Organisation und Rekursivität* Opladen, Westdt Verlag

Peters, F and Koch, J, eds (2004) *Integrierte erzieherische Hilfen: Flexibilität, Integration und Sozialraumbezug in der Jugendhilfe* Weinheim; München, Juventa-Verlag

Plake, K (1978) Umweltstrategien und Strukturprobleme der Sozialisationsorganisation *Soziale Welt*, 29:288-304

Rauschenbach, T (1990) Jugendhilfe als Arbeitsmarkt. In Peukert, D J K, ed, *Jugendhilfe Historischer Rückblick und neuere Entwicklungen*, Volume 1, p225-297 Weinheim; München, Juventa-Verlag Sachverständigenkommission 8 Jugendbericht (Hrsg)

Rauschenbach, T, Bendele, U, and Trede, W (1988) Mitarbeiter in der Jugendhilfe Struktur und Wandel des Personals in sozialen Diensten *Archiv für Wissenschaft und Praxis der sozialen Arbeit*, 19:163-190

Rauschenbach, T and Schilling, M (1997) Das Ende der Fachlichkeit? Soziale Berufe und die Personalstruktur im vereinten Deutschland *Neue Praxis*, 27:22-54

Reichard, C (1994) *Umdenken im Rathaus: Neue Steuerungsmodelle in der deutschen Kommunalverwaltung* Berlin, Ed Sigma

Sander, G (1988) Die Entwicklung der unterschiedlichen Betreuungsformen in der Heimerziehung unter Berücksichtigung der individualisierenden Hilfeformen Versuch einer Standortbestimmung der Heimerziehung – ein Beitrag zur Definition EREV *Fortbildungsbrief*, 29:422

Schilling, M (2001) Die Fachkräfte in den Erziehungshilfen In Birtsch, V, Münstermann, K, and Trede, W, eds, *Handbuch Erziehungshilfen Leitfaden für Ausbildung, Praxis und Forschung*, p458-487 Münster, Votum

Schimank, U (1995) Teilsystemevolutionen und Akteurstrategien: Die zwei Seiten struktureller Dynamiken moderner Gesellschaften *Soziale Systeme*, 1:73-100

Schrapper, C (1990) Voraussetzungen, Verlauf und Wirkungen der 'Heimkampagnen' *Neue Praxis*, 20:417-428

Schulz, G (1952-1966) Arten und Formen der Heime. In Trost, F, ed, *Handbuch der Heimerziehung*, p281-294 Frankfurt/Main; Berlin; Bonn; München, Diesterweg

Späth, K (1988) Die Entwicklung der unterschiedlichen Betreuungsformen in der Heimerziehung unter besonderer Berücksichtigung der individualisierenden Hilfeformen *EREV-Fortbildungsbrief*, 29:23-31

Späth, K (1989) Sozialpädagogische Tagesgruppen. In Blandow, J and Faltermeier, J, eds, *Erziehungshilfen in der Bundesrepublik Deutschland: Stand und Entwicklung*, p321-332 Stuttgart; Berlin; Köln; Mainz, Kohlhammer

Stephan, H (1985) Jugendwohngemeinschaft – 'Betreutes Wohnen' – Nachbetreuung *Unsere Jugend*, 37:262-266

Weick, K E and Bougon, M G (1986) Organizations as cognitive maps. In Sims, H P and Gioia, D A, eds, *The Thinking Organization*, p102-135 London, Jossey Bass

Wenzel, H (1970) *Fürsorgeheime in pädagogischer Kritik Eine Untersuchung in Heimen für männliche Jugendliche und Heranwachsende* Stuttgart, Klett

Wildavsky, A (1987) Choosing preferences by constructing institutions: a cultural theory of preference formation *American Political Science Review*, 81:321

Wolf, K (1995) Veränderungen in der Heimerziehungspraxis: Die großen Linien In Wolf, K, ed, *Entwicklungen in der Heimerziehung*, p12-64 Münster, Votum, Second edition

Wolf, K (1999) *Machtprozesse in der Heimerziehung: eine qualitative Studie über ein Setting klassischer Heimerziehung* Münster, Votum

Wolffersdorff, C von (1993) Wandel der Jugendhilfe – Mehr als nur ein Wort? *Neue Praxis*, 23:42-62

Wolffersdorff, C von, Sprau-Kuhlen, V, and Kersten, J (1996) *Geschlossene Un terbringung in Heimen: Kapitulation der Jugendhilfe?* Wein heim; München, Juventa-Verlag, Second edition

Zwischenbericht Kommission Heimerziehung (1977) *Heimerziehung und Alternativen: Analysen und Ziele für Strategien* Frankfurt/Main, Internationale Gesellschaft für Heimerziehung, Zwischenbericht Kommission Heimerziehung der Obersten Landesjugendbehörden und der Liga der Freien Wohlfahrtspflege

6

Transforming government services for children and families or 'Why non-reductionist policy, research and practice are almost too difficult to be tackled but too important to be left alone'[1]

James P. Anglin

This chapter engages with the issue of systemic change in child and family services. It concludes that at the root of our traditional helping services, and their frequent failure, is a fundamental misunderstanding of what it means to be human. The notion of the 'total human experiential moment', originally articulated by sociologist Dr. Robert Agger is explored and practical implications for practice, policy and research are suggested.

Introduction

While governments vary considerably in terms of their emphasis on universal, personal and developmental family provisions, most governments have sought to address family and child needs by creating departments and programmes to deliver various human services. If one looks at our systems in light of the functions families perform, it is evident that our health care system seeks to address the tasks of physical care and mental health intervention; our education system addresses a range of learning and socialisation tasks; income support and employment programmes relate to family consumption and economic tasks; justice services pertain to social control and the maintenance of order; and social services support the maintenance, substitution or restoration of family nurturing and motivation. We have, it appears, mirrored a number of key family functions within government structures.

On the face of it, this is a logical response to unmet individual and family needs which, if flexibly applied and modified over time as societal dynamics change (in theory at least) should be reasonably effective. However, it is evident from a survey of governments world-wide that there is an ongoing crisis in our human services systems. Calls for services that are truly 'integrated', 'multidisciplinary' and 'inter-sectoral' abound. The pleas for more holistic approaches and the overcoming of fragmentation at all levels first heard in a significant way in the 1960s and 1970s have over the past decade reached a crescendo, and there is a much stronger sense of urgency, almost desperation, in the calls for change and transformation.

Recently, governments in countries as divergent as the Netherlands, South Africa, United States and Canada have initiated major policy and programme design processes in an attempt to transform their traditional child and family services which they acknowledge do not work well. But can such attempts at transformation be successful? Why have our traditional services not been effective? This chapter seeks to uncover at least part of the answer to these important questions.

What exists, and how do we know it?

I have come to believe that fundamental to these pragmatic questions are issues of ontology and epistemology. I do not think we can avoid moving to considerations of what exists and how we know it if we truly wish to make some sense out of our current conceptual confusions and institutional crises. Basic to this position is a critique of the tendency to conceive of persons and families as divisible into parts, functions or needs, and of human life in general as divisible into discrete domains or sectors.

Abraham Maslow (1954) represents perhaps the best known example of this approach to understanding human beings. He posits a hierarchy of human needs, with certain needs being more basic than others. At the bottom of the hierarchy are the 'survival needs' for food, warmth and shelter. Above these are the needs for socialisation and companionship, then for aesthetic pursuits, and at the top of the pyramid is the need for self-actualisation.

To analyse human beings in this way, I suggest, is to put forward a model of the person as less than human. In reality, one cannot separate these levels. How one meets one's needs for food and shelter will be more or less self-actualising, more or less an aesthetically pleasing experience, and more or less a social event. For example, one may 'fuel the body-machine' in a solitary fashion at a fast food outlet or one may dine in style with friends at a gourmet restaurant. It is important to note that the entire so-called 'hierarchy of needs' is present in any and every particular situation, and each facet necessarily will be addressed in some way or other. Thus, to think about, or treat human beings as if their 'lower' needs can be addressed prior to, or in lieu of addressing their 'higher' needs is to dehumanise them and to treat them (for some purposes at least) as if they are mere animals or even objects. While Maslow's approach may be dated and out of vogue, it nevertheless appears to provide the implicit underpinnings for much of our current organisational reality.

In the area of individual functioning, it is commonplace to refer to various spheres or areas such as moral, intellectual, emotional, political, physical, social, economic, cultural, and spiritual. Because we are human beings, all these dimensions are present at all times. In making this point, sociologist Robert Agger (undated) has proposed the notion of the 'total human experiential moment' within which human life is lived as a whole. The concept of the total human experiential moment recognises that every human experience is characterised by wholeness. It is inaccurate and misleading to regard any human action as only an economic action, or only a political action, or only a nurturing action. Human experience, because it is human, is always multifaceted even though one or another facet may predominate in the moment.

A specific example used by Agger may be helpful to illustrate and clarify this assertion. The act of breastfeeding a child offers an excellent exemplar. Breastfeeding is a primal human experience in every sense of the word. It is an act that is initiated in the earliest moments and stages of human life and it pertains to the fundamental functions of being human. Further, it represents a critical, defining moment in both the development of family life and in setting the health trajectory for both the infant and the family as a whole. How should we describe and understand the act of a mother taking her baby to her breast, or turning away from the baby in rejection? This action presents a human situation that can perhaps help us to clarify some of the key current issues related to family services, and to families in general, whether we approach these phenomena as researchers, policy makers or practitioners.

To many people, breastfeeding is simply an act of providing sustenance. To baby formula companies, breastfeeding is essentially provisioning, and offers an economic opportunity from which they can benefit monetarily. And yet, the act of breastfeeding is also intrinsically a matter of social relations. The mother is demonstrating affection for the child, and is stimulating the beginnings of such relating on the part of the infant. Further, this act is also intrinsically one of influence, of power. The mother has the power to give or withhold her breast, her milk and her affection, and the child may engage in tactics, perhaps instinctive and not fully conscious at first, such as crying and flailing about in order to influence the mother.

Thus, in this primal human experience reside the basic elements of politics and governance – who gets what, when and how. The infant experiences what can be termed the 'political style' of the mother, whether it is a benevolent or malevolent dictatorship, authoritarian, or a loving democracy. This analysis could be extended equally to all facets of the breastfeeding experience as a total human experience such as morality, education, justice, and so on.

I believe that if we are to be truly successful in achieving the kinds of transformations in government services and family life that are being called for today from all directions, we need to ground our thinking and actions in this basic ontological truth, namely that every human experience is a totality which can be described and understood in terms of all facets of human development and human relations. It is a reality, a fact of life, given that we are human beings. To be human is to be a whole person with multiple, if not infinite, facets.

Yet I am aware that most of our lives are spent experiencing ourselves and others as if we are less than fully human. We tend to think of ourselves and others as partial human subjects, conscious of one or perhaps two facets to our being at any given moment. Our societal institutions and organisations are conceived, organised and operated on the premise of partialised being. In our more reflective moments, or when we are engaging each other more fully as persons, likely away from the dominant presence of institutional settings, we may lament the dehumanising power of our institutions, yet we feel powerless to change this reality. I believe that the current call for integration of services, for multi-disciplinary teamwork, for a client-centred approach, for systems transformation, and for a new paradigm of social development needs to be understood as a cry from the heart from people who are witnessing and experiencing the pains of disintegration, isolation, disempowerment, and an overall sense of organisational insensitivity and impotence in relation to real human experiences and situations.

In summary, we as policy makers, practitioners and researchers must shift our thinking and actions away from partial and therefore dehumanising responses to people's situations, and we must exert our influence to ensure that the total human experience of each and every person is acknowledged and responded to with true sensitivity and empathy.

This is a tall order, and brings us face to face with the fact that powerful forces, including entrenched beliefs, values and habits of mind and behaviour, are working against such an approach. It has been a defining characteristic of our modern era that people have perceived themselves and each other as partial subjects, or even as objects. To paraphrase the famous dictum of American, W.I. Thomas, 'When people perceive situations to be real, they are real in their consequences'. This appears to be one of the major roadblocks to social trans-formation. If we perceive human situations and experiences as partial and fragmented when they are in reality whole and undifferentiated, we will create institutions and professional responses, including public policies, research studies, and professional practices that treat people and situations as parts and fragments rather than as whole, integrated entities. The reality of these inadequate and misguided responses then reinforces the distorted per-ceptions, and we find ourselves locked into an endless cycle of dehumanisa-tion both for the clients and the specialists. Is there a way to break out of this pattern?

The way ahead

I think the first step is to take seriously the severity of the problem and the need for change. Even if we as professionals are relatively comfortable and accustomed to acting in fragmented ways, it is clear that the impact on many of our targets, be they research subjects, communities or clients, is far from acceptable and satisfactory.

Second, we must recognise the negative impacts of our existing constructs, frameworks and language which reinforce the illusion that people and situations are divisible into domains, parts, sectors and areas. In general, much of our technical and professional language is inaccurate, faulty and destructive of personal integrity. Our research, policy development and pro-fessional practice activities consist of sets of people interacting with each other within sets of operations defined and guided by language consisting of concepts, frameworks and grammar. We need to remind ourselves con-tinually that in every institution in which we work, with each dedicated to a discrete facet of the human situation, there exists the full range of other facets characteristic of the total human experience even though the participants, both the clients and the specialists, are not conscious of experiencing them or engaging with them.

One strategy that can begin the process of change is to treat as one category what have previously been treated as separate and discrete categories. An example of this strategy used by the author is the concept of 'educational training'. Traditionally, much effort has been put into trying to differentiate and separate these two notions, 'education' versus 'training', and entire learning systems and organisations have been put into place to reflect these supposed separate realities. In reality, these are two facets of learning that are best addressed together within many holistic learning paradigms and programmes.

Third, the way ahead in human services seems to call for an opening up of our institutional life to more people's experiences, more points of view, and more voices. Existing organisations tend to be characterised by a spurious precision of language and purpose – often referred to as 'mandate' – which hides or disguises the everyday realities experienced by people. More of the total human experiences of people who practise in specialised roles need to connect with the experiences of those they serve or with whom they work in order to create a more integrated and total, and therefore truly human, experience for all participants.

Implications for practice, policy and research

In relation to the specific (but not discrete) functions of practice, policy and research, I suggest the following. In the area of practice (which contains important facets of policy and research), we must remain vitally concerned with the human experiences of the whole persons who become enveloped by the institutions in which we work, including most fundamentally ourselves.

We need to seek first to access and understand the lived experience of those we are there to serve. The most effective way to accomplish this is to participate together in joint ventures so that both parties can develop renewed and transformed understandings of each other and the nature of their mutual involvement. In such an interactive and mutual process, the language of the activity, traditionally quite technical and partial, is shifted in order to refer more accurately to real, lived experiences, problems and aspirations. As Alfred North Whitehead has observed, 'We think in generalities but we live in details'.

A large step forward will be taken if we can stop putting energy into trying to solve pseudo-problems or in reinforcing a false ontology through our words and actions. Put another way, we have to stop doing what we know doesn't work in order to create a space in which we can discover what can work.

In the field of policy (which contains important facets of practice and research), we need to transform our concepts, frameworks and language in order to enable community-building and the opening-up of institutions. As with practice, we should refrain from taking positions and trying to solve problems that can be better addressed by those more informed and experienced at the appropriate levels in the system. Policy can play an important role in mandating processes involving a much broader range of persons and their perspectives, and granting them voices and meaningful representation in decision-making.

In research – which contains important facets of policy and practice – similar issues of perspective and participation need to be addressed. A rather unorthodox definition of research method offered by Marie Jahoda is relevant. She suggests to the social science researcher to 'read as much as you can, think as much as you can, take on (in imagination at least) as many points of view involved in the situation as possible as a participant, and trust to the higher powers that the answer will come' (Jahoda, 1988). This wisdom comes from an eminent researcher with over fifty years of research experience, and should not be dismissed as too folksy to be taken seriously. I believe her understanding of the research enterprise well reflects the complex, multi-faceted reality of human experience and implies that a participative and multi-perspectival human experiential approach to research will be most likely to reveal the real nature of human and social situations being investigated.

Conclusion

The quest for non-reductionist language, strategies and actions is almost too difficult to be tackled but too important not to be pursued. While I have tried to suggest some small steps in this direction, perhaps the most important preparation for this task is for each of us, whether we are working as researchers, policy makers or practitioners, to seek to expand our self-awareness, our understandings, and our abilities to act towards others as whole persons.

It is evident that much of the response we bring forward from others is directly related to what we are able to put out toward to them. The onus, then, is on us as professionals to reach out first with genuineness and true respect, even if our role is not a care-giving or therapeutic one.

My own research (Anglin, 2002) has led me to believe that congruence is of vital importance in human service work at all levels and across all functions.

We must strive to treat our co-workers with as much respect as we believe parents ought to treat each other; we must attend to governmental policy-making processes with the same care for others that we would want demonstrated in family meetings; we must engage our research subjects with the same genuineness and honesty we expect from those with whom we live and work. In brief, an essential element of a non-reductionist approach is to think, experience and act in full recognition of the integrity of persons and the wholeness of human life.

Note

1 I wish to acknowledge the important work of Dr. Robert Agger whose draft manuscript, shared with me over 25 years ago, has made a deep and lasting impression on my thinking. His insightful development of the notion of the 'total human experiential moment' and his analysis of potential implications for society have been drawn upon here in an attempt to understand and articulate their applicability to contemporary practice, policy and research relating to services for children and families. I owe the alternate title of this paper to Dr. Marie Jahoda, a British social psychologist who wrote a marvellous article entitled Why a non-reductionist social psychology is almost too difficult to be tackled but too fascinating to be left alone (Jahoda, 1989).

References

Agger, R E (Undated) How to end the divisions of labour and life. Unpublished document

Anglin, J P (2002) *Pain, normality and the struggle for congruence: reinterpreting residential care for children and youth* Binghampton NY, Haworth

Jahoda, M (1988) Personal communication. Lecture at the Department of Experimental Psychology, Oxford University, England

Jahoda, M (1989) Why a non-reductionist social psychology is almost too difficult to be tackled but too fascinating to be left alone *British Journal of Social Psychology*, 28:71-78

Maslow, A H (1954) *Motivation and Personality* New York, Harper and Row

Professional and research perspectives
on a changing world of residential child
and youth care

7

The professionalisation of child and youth care practice: Professionalising social pedagogy – from practice to theory and back to practice

Alenka Kobolt and Bojan Dekleva

'Our children are citizens of today and tomorrow's society; supporting children is a long-term assignment and an investment of society.' (Ministrstvo za delo, družino in socialne zadeve, 2003)

Introduction

The quotation is from the programme inspired by the document *A World Fit for Children* (United Nations General Assembly, 2002). It was prepared by the Ministry of Work, Family and Social Affairs together with the Slovenian Council for Children and UNICEF for the period between 2003 and 2013.

The document highlights, among other factors, the necessity of a healthy life start for all children, access to health services, the promotion of a healthy lifestyle, access to quality, free education and, above all, protection from cruelty and discrimination. It sets realistic, measurable goals for future inclusion in legal documents as well as in national and local social programmes. The programme discussed was drawn up with the idea that its goals would be realised through the implementation of the actions proposed. However, discrepancies between the said plans and everyday life still remain.

Social consciousness of the problems faced by today's young people can be a contradictory process. On the one hand, formal and informal social commitment to young people and other vulnerable social groups is on the increase. This can be seen in the various new documents concerning acts, action plans and regulations all over Europe. However, despite the special attention given to those with social integration problems, it is no longer possible to speak solely about specific groups of vulnerable/at risk young people, because vulnerability and deprivation can easily become a reality for any young human being who may fail to fit social norms and who may then suffer fundamentally as a result. In spite of this, the paper focuses on the vulnerable groups of children and youngsters whose upbringing requires the support and special attention of society in the form of intervention by social workers and special needs teachers – professionals who have much in common and work in the same field of psychosocial support and help. There are different traditions in the way these terms are used. We use the term 'social pedagogue' as a broader term which covers the fields of social work, social care and education.

Professionalisation and development in the field

The residential care of children and young people who lack appropriate family care and have difficulties involving social integration is undoubtedly the oldest element in the wider field of social pedagogy[1]. Nohl claimed that 'The field of social pedagogy is everything which is education but including neither family nor school' (Thiersch and Rauschenbach, 1987, p974). On the basis of this understanding, Thiersch defines social pedagogy as '... a scientific social theory about child and youth care, whereby the tasks, contents and perspectives of the discipline are set within the context of development and implementation of care and are directly linked to the historical and social structures' (*op cit*, p987).

As a professional discipline, social pedagogy is placed within three interdependent relational directions: the first is the relationship between theory and practice, so that the theory has to seek answers to the open questions of practice, the second refers to the understanding of practice within the framework of general educational and social goals, tasks and realities of modern times, and the third is marked by the link between social pedagogy and the wider social historical context.

Winkler (2003) used the metaphor for the connection between the theory and practice as a relation of the basement (practice) and the first floor (theory), whereby the latter should reflect the problems emerging from the basement/ practice – ie the everyday life of users. This should be understood as a problem not only individually but also socially generated and one where pedagogical intervention is no longer sufficient to address the problem. The continuum of intervention required within the profession is expanding together with the problems it encounters.

The key elements constituting the field and setting it off as a theoretically and professionally distinct discipline are: scientific research with reflection and links between research, theoretical summarising and innovations of practical applications, the existence of formal educational programmes at higher education or university level and the professional community with a clearly formed ethical code.

A short illustration of the above elements – the case of Slovenia

The early ideas and theoretical foundations of pedagogy and special and residential care were brought to Slovenia chiefly through the work of Austrian and German teachers in the mid-nineteenth century. Further development in residential care came after the Second World War and, later, via research at the Institute of Criminology at the Faculty of Law. Yet further development of the social pedagogy educational programme materialised, at higher (1965) and, later at university level (1989)[2]. These developments ensured that social pedagogy is a recognised profession. There is no order of priority, since the individual elements interconnect developmentally and with regard to society and are mutually interdependent.

Although Slovenia was a relatively closed country after the Second World War, theory and practice resumed, oriented towards Europe, in the 1950s (Skalar, 1988). New theoretical models were included in research projects and then applied to practice (the democratisation of the education (1967), new concepts and the normalisation of living conditions in residential institutions (1985 and later), and programmes of the NGOs which were established only in the late 1980s). The series of studies were interconnected and resulted in a reflection of the educational practice up to the present (Dekleva, 1985; Dekleva, 1993; Kobolt, 1998a; Sket, 1993).

The next element of the profession is defined as practical performance, professional cooperation and reflection within the framework of the professional community with a well-formed ethical code. In contemporary Slovenia, the professional community is organised first and foremost into special and rehabilitation pedagogues who work predominantly in the institutionalised out-of-home care, while the Association for Social Pedagogy links to all other fields of practical activities – prevention, kindergarten and school work, youth work, integrative work with all marginal groups and other integrative projects.

Between the theory and the practice – from past to present

At their first conference in Paris, 78 years ago, European pioneers of social work were already asking themselves about the key areas of knowledge that social, child and youth care workers and similar professions should acquire in order to deal with the problems encountered. Moltzer, from the Social School in Amsterdam in 1928, said, 'Especially sociology has the danger of being too abstract. The student should not be enabled to give an abstract review of the theory but to know its effects on the economic life of a working-class family', and ended with, 'We have summarised a large group of basic social subjects: all sciences that directly refer to people...' (Seibel, 1996, p28).

His words acknowledge the need for reflective and applicable knowledge. At the same time, it is obvious that even in those pioneering times the mapped knowledge covered a broad range of subjects. The goals of social and child care work today remain in line with this tradition. In the first place there is the assistance to individuals who, in the contemporary, postmodern, globalised society, find themselves in marginal situations. Their coping strategies, acquired knowledge and skills and their social and economic resources are insufficient to attain a satisfying personal and social way of life. Consequently, there is still an obvious need to understand the social and cultural contexts of users, as some notable published titles can prove: '*La misere du monde – Das Elend der Welt*' (Bourdieu *et al*, 1993), *Community: Seeking safety in an insecure world* (Baumann, 2001), '*Identität und Bindung*' (Garlichs and Leuziner-Bohleber, 1999), '*Developing culturally sensitive services*' (Zaviršek and Flaker, 1995), '*Zur Professionalität in integrierten, flexiblen Hilfen*' (Peters and Wolff, 1997).

We agree with Lorenz that workers in social occupations in Europe today need 'principles and methods which make diversity count as an asset to societies and which above all give people on the margins of society the means of defining their own sense of belonging' (1996, p41).

In the document on the common platform for social educators in Europe social educational work is understood as 'a process of social actions in relation to individuals and various groups of individuals whereby their methods are multidimensional and include: Care, education, intervention, treatment, development of non-exclusive life space treatment etc. The goal is full sociability and citizenship to all.' (Association internationale des éducateurs sociaux, 2005). A similar direction for child and youth care work was the goal of the Neurim Declaration (FICE Expert Seminar, 1991) designed by representatives of FICE fourteen years earlier.

Describing the profile of child and youth care worker S. Vernooij (1995) classifies the required competence into the following areas:

* personal competence – becoming aware of one's own values, prejudices, emotional responses, expectations, strengths and weaknesses;

* theoretical knowledge – additionally to the general knowledge a special mastering of various interventions;

* competence of an analytic understanding of situations in education, family life, peer groups etc, requiring the recognition of social situations, one's own perceptive mechanisms, recognition of conflict situations and the ability to solve them;

* competent action which is not only a highly ethical intervention, but also a willingness to seek individual solutions for those who use the service.

Competent actions require synthesis of knowledge from different areas such as understanding the individual's development, group leadership, relationships and interaction among systems, counselling and therapy competence. Social pedagogical work requires quick responses and autonomous decision-making in a constant search for creative ways to solve everyday problems.

The document: *A common platform for social educators in Europe* was published by the European Bureau of the International Association of Social Educators. The Bureau was set up with the aim 'to set criteria applied to professional qualifications that attest to a sufficient level of competence for the purpose of practising a given profession...' (Association internationale des éducateurs sociaux, 2005, p3). The document highlights some of the main guidelines and requirements for the practice and training for this profession, 'The work is based on the UN Universal Declaration of Human Rights, and presupposed a fundamental understanding of the integrity and value of each single human being, irrespective of race, gender, age, belief, social and economical and intellectual status in the society' (Association internationale des éducateurs sociaux, 2005, p5).

As previously mentioned, the profession is rooted in the humanities, based on several disciplines and has an integrating view of knowledge as a central principle, so the competence of workers should be characterised as a synthesis of knowledge, skills and attitudes. The same document (2005, p2) defines three fundamental and six central competences for this work. The fundamental competences are: competence in intervention, evaluation and reflection, and the central competences are: personal and relational, organisational, system, development and learning competence. The last group forms competences generated by professional practice which are connected with ethical demands and principles.

Among the competences generated by the practice are: theoretical knowledge and methodical competence, codes of conduct within the profession and, last but not least, cultural and creative competence. Let us describe the last two. Creative competence is understood as the mastering of various forms of expression and skills within creativity and as collaboration with the users in such ways that these activities acquire and develop their own form of expression and extension of creative horizons in a social and cultural context. Cultural competence has several dimensions: knowing and recognising the cultural values of the users, being able to understand and reflect the different cultures of the users and also of the institutions and professionals they are involved with (Association internationale des éducateurs sociaux, 2005).

At present there is a major debate on the competences and various views about the meaning of this term. Debate aside, we can conclude that the crucial areas of competence – the main core of the social pedagogical work – are the promotion of supportive relations and situations where the users will be able to discover and strengthen the personal potential within the individual, group and social intervention processes, in order to achieve a satisfactory level of life skills.

Müller claims that

> Social pedagogues are experts in the fields of human services – but it's hard to tell what kind of experts. They are doing 'social work': in foster homes, youth programs, schools, ambulant services or places for the disabled. They are paid, among other things, for educating kids with some difficulties and for helping them and their families out of trouble – but what is exactly the professional service and competence they are paid for? If one compares them to other human service professions like doctors and therapists, lawyers or teachers it is obvious that their area of competence is somewhat vague and less well defined. (1998, p76)

He posed the relevant question of whether social pedagogues can really be competent for 'the whole' complexity of modern life. He proposes the answer that competent social pedagogues should be 'well informed citizens' amongst other things, and should possess some specific areas of competence. To illustrate 'competence' he uses the metaphor of 'settlers' and 'wilderness guides'. The competence of 'settlers' can be found among doctors, lawyers or therapists. The competence of the 'wilderness guides' includes flexibility and being able to work in circumstances of uncertainty.

Müller wrote that social pedagogues ...

> are notoriously confronted with a host of problems on different levels which is a
> wilderness in itself. They cannot solve or even understand these problems all at
> once; they cannot pull a fence around them and say, 'We will solve them one by
> one'. They get entangled into them, and they almost inevitably drift into situations of
> 'helpless helpers'. (1998, p80)

Stability in continuous interpersonal relations remains the cornerstone of
this profession. It requires the understanding of interpersonal relationships
and the social relations whereby the practitioner is using 'his/her own body
and mind' (Association internationale des éducateurs sociaux, 2005, p6),
which requires self-knowledge, self-awareness and reflection. Simple solutions to individual and social problems no longer exist. This is also true of
doctrines and canons in the social pedagogical profession. More and more,
they are being replaced by the idea of a reflective practitioner who should be
able to contribute flexibly to the process of development of innovative solutions in each single case with the participation of all parties involved (Dekleva
et al, 2006).

Child and youth care from the European point of view

Some common characteristics can be observed in the development of
residential care in Europe but also many differences. Similarities are apparent
in the policy of integrating flexible, individually-shaped measures in the
everyday context of the users' lives: day care, work within families, integrative
and flexible intervention designed on the basis of the individual needs.
Similarities can also be seen in the trends occurring within care: short-term
placements, social inclusion, various models of care and their integration
into the social environment and vice versa. This relatively synchronous
development, taking into consideration the main trends, is astonishing since
the international organisations for out-of-home care – FICE (International
Federation of Educative Communities) and the World Association of Youth
Care Workers are among just a few of the world-wide professional connections. When making more in-depth micro-analysis, the low level of congruity
or comparison between different countries is revealed (Trede, 2001). However, in all European countries greater professionalisation can be seen in
social pedagogy, social education and other care work.

Comparative studies dealing with this field even in the past, (Gottesman,
1991, 1994) reveal an agreement about the most important issue: high quality
service. This translates as competent personnel and suitable living and working standards, which together enable intensive personal relationships which

remain the main working tool of care workers. It is agreed that professionals need constant professional training in the form of tutoring, practical counselling and supervision. However, within the area of social care policy there exists much more agreement about common standards than is evident in practice, because of the different state of development in different countries. Among the educational programmes in the field there was, and still is, everything from in-service training of short duration to university masters and doctoral programmes, carried out in the name of social pedagogy or social work or special education (Jones, 1993).

The practical approach to education and social care seems to be driven by the spectrum of scientific and practical everyday theories and basic concepts. In everyday situations the professional has to adapt to the needs of the individual in question. Attention should be given to the conditions and limitations that originate from the functional limits of the institutions. Time and cost pressures, although they may awaken new creativity in both the professionals and the users, are also significant. This is why care professions are classified at the level of semi-professions (compare Vander Ven and Tittnich, 1986). In spite of the dilemmas and obstacles, the future development of the field and the growing demands on the professionals are inevitable.

What contributes to quality?

Within the field of human services quality has become an important subject of discussion. The popularity of the topic presents as an opportunity to evaluate and redefine the categories, self-evident until now, and to implement innovations and to rise above the level of semi-professionalisation.

Compared with the other caring professions, special teachers, social educators, care workers, social workers and social pedagogues exhibit additional dimensions. Educational and care work represents not only teaching but demands the creation of the whole life context of the service users, including everything from physical care – nutrition, and accommodation – to the structuring of spare time and appropriate activities.

This ensures that opportunities exist in which to satisfy the needs of deprived and marginalised groups, performing supportive as well as therapeutic intervention. If those groups or individuals are to gain from the work and the relationship established with the professionals, they need to become better equipped to understand the process of social integration and the rights of every individual. The discouraging influences originating from the individual's own life circumstances, family or social sphere within the wider and immediate environment which resulted in their requiring assistance in the first place need to be understood and transformed with great sensitivity and professional ethics.

In the past, attention within professional circles was focused on the service users' problems in context, but recently more attention has been paid to the analysis of the professional work and the qualifications it requires. It is important to take into account the planning, content and manner of implementation of the study programmes for later use within those professions.

Three interconnected groups of factors contribute to better child and youth care:

- A varied and flexible continuum of offers available to users – models ranging from preventive forms integrated into regular education, short- and long-term projects, various models of group homes and flexible out-of-home care;

- Quality assurance in the above mentioned models – factors related to work organisation, setting standards, educational management, team development intervention, leading to the creation of suitable life conditions. Supervision in various forms enables professional reflection, ensuring support for the individual's and team's professional development, improving communication among team members and understanding users' needs (Kobolt, 1998; Zorga, 1997).

- A well formed study programme, shaping the workers' future professional and personal identity. In addition to research and the existence of professional community training programs, there is a third element of professionalism, as claimed by Vander Ven and Tittnich (1986). A wide range of training programmes is available, from short-term in-service training to university programmes, all of them offered under the name of social pedagogy and/or social work.

Contribution of study to the quality and professionalisation of the work

How can study contribute to the quality of child and youth care? University study programmes for the profession worldwide include three fundamental elements: theoretical knowledge, practical skills and self-knowledge. It is only by knowing and mastering all three that action will be competent, ethical and professional. Jones (1992) compared similar programmes in various European countries and discovered an astounding concordance of the subject matter, although there are relevant differences in the levels of prescribed education.

The common characteristics are: involvement in the social context, interdisciplinary conception of programmes enabling insight into society and groups and also into the individual as well as the personal contribution of the professional. The Slovene university programme tries to link the above mentioned premises. If the aim of a programme is to train students by delivering adequate knowledge and supporting their personal development, it needs to help them become responsible for their own professional development. So their voices, opinions and needs have to be listened to and taken into account.[3]

Present practice is based on decades of development of theoretical concepts within the field of social sciences. It requires an interdisciplinary and team approach. Since the study programme is the first step into the profession, it should fulfil the following requirements:

■ Its content should include a basic knowledge of human development within a social context, together with an understanding of the interaction required as specific knowledge of various methods and interventions.

■ Methodically it should be formed in so as to enable the students' active participation, collaboration and reflection about how they function.

Evaluating the Slovene University study programme

We applied two methods of evaluation. In the first the study programme was evaluated by 120 full-time students (referred to as regular students below) and 47 part-time students (already working in the field, and referred to as field work students). In total 167 students enrolled in the social pedagogy programme at the Faculty of Education in Ljubljana between 1997 and 2003. The evaluation included seven generations of full-time students and two generations of part-time students, because this type of study is available only every four years. The students were all in their seventh semester, ensuring that their study experience was of equal duration. Due to space limitations the results are presented selectively. In the second evaluation in the year 2004/2005 the competence questionnaire was implemented within the course, and the responses of the 55 already graduated social pedagogues, postgraduate students and academics were gained.[4]

Key results as given by students in the evaluation questionnaire

The students' replies about what they gained from the programme are grouped into three sections:

Theoretical knowledge

- Widened horizons: statements about usefulness of the study in the sense of widening one's ways of thinking about work-related questions ('I found the wide context of the social pedagogy programme especially useful' ... 'widening my horizons').

- Developed cognitive processes: statements about being able to think, to develop one's ways of thinking, analysing, understanding, synthesising connecting topics ('opportunity to discuss problems'...'I liked those courses where it was necessary to think a lot' ... 'I spent more time thinking about life and I looked for reasons why things happen').

- Understanding the world around them: statements about understanding the dynamics of relationships in social systems – family, school, society ('I can explain relationships in the family').

Skills and learning through experience

- Learned through experience: statements about learning based on practical experience, tutorials, voluntary work, field work, visits to institutions, project learning ('visiting institutions' ... 'experiential learning' ... 'I found the tutorials useful' 'in the first year I liked the team seminars').

- Acquired new skills: this category included replies about the usefulness of the study programme in the sense of acquiring and developing communication skills, conflict resolving skills etc ('communication skills').

Work on oneself, experiential training and project work

- Worked on oneself: this category includes statements on activities leading to a better knowledge of oneself, one's feelings, responses, views, abilities, progress etc ('I've learnt to accept differences better' 'breaking up prejudices').

- Project work: connection with the practice which enables one to reflect on oneself, one's abilities, limits, coping strategies ('voluntary work enabled me to connect theory with practice').

Knowledge gained and skills for the work domains of social pedagogues

Social pedagogy has spread from traditional residential institutions to a wider area of child and youth work, including preventive projects, different models of day care, school counselling, work with minority groups (gypsies, immigrants), the elderly, community work. Here is the answer to the question of how students felt about their professional skills when faced with these challenges.

Table 1: I feel I am well trained for the following jobs:

	Regular students	Field work students
GROUP WORK		
with children	85.0%	72.5%
with youngsters	92.0%	58.5%
with adults	23.0%	54.0%
TYPE OF WORK		
organising and leading	45.0%	64.0%
counselling	52.0%	64.5%
WORK DOMAIN		
residential care	76.5%	34.8%
work in school	93.0%	82.0%
kindergarten	48.0%	68.0%
social agency	52.0%	58.0%
prison	31.0%	15.0%
NGO projects	64.0%	33.0%

Regular students perceived themselves to be sufficiently trained for group work with children and adolescents but insufficiently for working with adults. They thought they needed further knowledge and skills to be able to organise, lead, and counsel. This could be because both courses were in the last year of the study programme, which they had not yet completed. They felt that they were adequately trained for work in schools and residential settings, but not for work in kindergartens or social agencies, and even less for work in prisons. They felt slightly more adequately trained for work in non-governmental organisations which, in Slovenia, are a relatively recent development.

Achieved (required) and preferred competences

In the year 2004/2005, 55 students, practitioners and academics answered questionnaires about the competence a social pedagogue should possess and on general competence. Only the results on specific competences are shown here, illustrating the present and the desired level of specific competences.

Table 2: Ranks of present and preferred (desired) level of competence

Ranking specific competences	Mark	Present rank	Desired mark	Desired rank
empathy and open communication	3.3091	1	3.87	1
understanding the processes of stigmatisation, marginalisation, social exclusion and prevention thereof	3.1273	2	3.78	4
understanding and acceptance of diversity as a quality, acceptance of other cultures and subcultures; ability in non-stigmatisation work	3.1111	3	3.74	8
knowledge and critical understanding of various deviant phenomena	3.0909	5	3.78	5
knowledge of theoretical bases of social work and child care work and their practical application	3.0909	4	3.71	11
ability to reflect one's own involvement in work with people, ability to take responsibility for own professional development, willingness for supervision and intervision forms of work	3.0182	6	3.87	2
knowledge, understanding and consideration of the individual through the prism of different theoretical models	2.9630	7	3.48	20
educational and counselling work with individuals and groups within institutions	2.8000	8	3.75	6
understanding various forms of personal and social violence and their causes	2.7636	9	3.75	7
professional work oriented to the user's life sphere, ability of work in the existing social circumstances	2.6727	10	3.73	9
understanding of institutional function, institutional influence on users, evaluation of one's own institutional involvement	2.6481	11	3.51	17

Key: The scale from 1 to 4 is given as the frame for marking the level of the competence

Table 2: Ranks of present and preferred (desired) level of competence (cont)

Ranking specific competences	Mark	Present rank	Desired mark	Desired rank
understanding and implementation of various types of social pedagogical work (preventive, educational, counselling, social integrative, etc)	2.6000	12	3.82	3
ability to assess the quality and potential in the individual's social networks (family, neighbourhood, institutional cooperation, etc)	2.5273	13	3.51	18
outreach, ambulant and community based work	2.4727	14	3.65	13
cooperative work in interdisciplinary teams, projects, analytical and evaluation groups	2.4182	15	3.64	14
cooperation and work with parents, families and other important service users' social groups	2.3636	16	3.69	12
ability to make an appropriate individual programme for help, support, intervention	2.2727	17	3.73	10
preparation, leading and evaluation of special pedagogic projects (voluntary or preventive work, advocacy work, self-help groups, etc)	2.2727	18	3.64	15
analytical and research work in the area of social pedagogy for the needs of practice development	2.0000	19	3.49	19
social marketing activities (introduction and promotion of social pedagogical principles in the public arena)	1.5818	20	3.53	16

Key: The scale from 1 to 4 is given as the frame for marking the level of the competence

The main competence has the same rank in the existing and the desired level. It is in empathy and open communication. All the others differ a little (1 or 2) up to 7, 9, or even 13 ranks. There are also small differences in competence areas such as orientation into the life context of users with the ability to work in existing social circumstances, team work in projects, analytical and evaluation groups. The difference is minimal in understanding the following: the process of stigmatisation and social exclusion, educational and counselling work with individuals and groups, and the understanding of violent behaviour and its causes. A marked difference is apparent in the understanding of the individual through different theoretical models. Here the discrepancy is the result of the existing level being higher (7) than the desired one (20). For the programme staff this can be an indication to seek different ways to translate such theoretical knowledge into practice. A high discrepancy also shows competence in being able to distinguish among different models of work – preventive, supportive, compensating – (12) which needs to be much higher (3). Better planning is also required to provide the appropriate intervention and to be able to work with families and parents of a children or young people.

Conclusions and implications for future developments

The study programme provides a satisfactory spectrum of theoretical knowledge and skills through which the students can understand the dynamics of relationships within different social systems as well as be aware of their own involvement in the social processes. Nevertheless, some of the regular full-time and part-time students still need additional theoretical knowledge. This can be interpreted as suitable motivation for the continuation of professional development (permanent education) but could also confirm the view that theoretical knowledge is over-emphasised. We see this in the discrepancy between the rank of the acquired and preferred competence: understanding and considering the individual through the prism of different theoretical models. The first is ranked seventh while the desired level of competence ranked last, in 20th place.

The evaluation clearly shows that the programme does not focus on self-evaluation and work on oneself. This is an important outcome, particularly when considering the relationship as an integral part of the child and youth care profession. The professional/service user relationship is shaped by the professional's identity, inclinations, attitudes and motivation. Our study programme appears to have neglected this crucial aspect. How can it be better integrated in the future? Mostly by a different method of delivering the theoretical and practical contents, so there is more focus on personal, relational and practical aspects.

The lack of applicability is most prominent in the second part of this evaluation, which deals with the levels of acquired and preferred (desired) competence areas. These differ significantly in the category of appropriation. For instance, the competence 'understanding and implementation of various types of social pedagogical work (preventive, educational, counselling, social integrative work)', ranked twelfth on the acquired competence dimension and third on the preferred. The competence 'being able to make an appropriate individual programme for help, support, and intervention' similarly scored seventeenth on the acquired and tenth on the desired level of competence. These emphases demonstrate that the knowledge acquired lacks applicability.

How could this be improved on in future? We propose active study methods and project work. Project work is where students experience have greatest potential for self-understanding, by testing their practical skills and attitudes within their studies. Individual work and team-work oriented study programmes would enable them to acquire knowledge and skills in planning, execution and managing processes and to transfer the acquired experience to other fields of study. This competence is the one which is desired most, yet achieved least.

Child and youth care work is about working in a team. According to students, there is not enough interaction and cooperation among the tutors providing the study programme. To us as tutors this feedback proves very valuable. If we truly want our students to be prepared and well equipped for team-work we should set an example. We should contribute to their sensitivity for team-work by demonstrating cooperation among ourselves. Another shortcoming of the evaluated study programme is the narrow choice of optional study courses. The remodelling of the programme according to the requirements of the Bologna process will resolve this problem, since the process guidelines prescribe a mandatory share of courses to choose from. This will result in a tailor-made study programme suited to individual students. Finally, the evaluation results suggest a more practical approach to knowledge transfer, which has been, until now, restricted by the organisational principles of the University programme.

Notes

1 The term 'social pedagogy' is already 150 years old. This is a truly respectable age, as are also the contributions of several authors, with Magers as the first to use this term as far back as 1844 (Winkler, 1988, p41). Magers defined social pedagogy as a theoretical discipline dealing with evaluation, description and questions about the real educational processes carried out at a certain place in a certain time. In 1949/50 Diesterweg (Winkler, 2003) used the same expression and defined it as a discipline dealing with changed situations experienced by the young, and also included research of the relationships within social and educational dimensions.

2 With the programme, which had been designed following similar programmes around the world (Germany, Canada, Denmark) and which took into account features and special conditions characteristic of the Slovene setting, we gained not only competent personnel with university education, which strengthened the profession, but also new possibilities for the classification of the profile. Rapid social changes, in recent decades are reflected in the changed conditions of practical work and in new theoretical and research challenges. Social pedagogy will be able to meet these challenges if, in accordance with tradition, it succeeds in linking innovations from practice with theoretical reflections, and if all the efforts of research and practice are consistently applied to the life settings of the addressees.

3 Working areas of the Slovene social pedagogues can be illustrated also through the content of the Third Congress, organised by the national professional community – *Združenje za Socialno pedagogiko* (Rogla, 2005, in Klemenčič, (2005), with the title 'Models of best practice in social-pedagogical work – professional challenges in the post-modern society of uncertainty'. It aimed to give space for the presentation of models of best practice and to facilitate dialogue. The contributions were presented in the following Congress sections/symposia: Social education and social capital, School counselling work, Vulnerable social groups and unemployment, Drug use and harm reduction, Community mental health, Challenges for an inclusive society in times of global migrations, Street work, Placing children and youth in residential institutions, Penal and post-penal work, Work with families, Juvenile delinquency – alternative sanctions and measures, Community work – challenges in the society of uncertainty, Children and youth residential care in future, Public health issues, Management of non-profit organisations in the field of social pedagogy.

4 Sample for the first evaluation

Evaluation questionnaire: The entire sample of 167 students is divided into two groups:

Group 1 – UG – Undergraduate students – full time students – year of evaluation, number of included students: year 1997 – N 19; year 1998 – N 28; year 1999 – N 21; year 2000 – N 17; year 2001 – N 13; year 2002 – N 10; year 2003 – N 12 – total 120 students.

Group 2 – FW – field work students – part time students graduated from other high schools, having field work experience in various settings – kindergarten, school, social work etc.

Year of evaluation, number of included students: year 1999 – N 33, year 2003 – N 14, total 47.

Sample for the second evaluation

55 graduate social pedagogues, postgraduate students and academics

References

Association internationale des éducateurs sociaux (2005) *A Common Platform for Social Educators in Europe* Barcelona, European Office of the International Association of Social Educators (EOAIEJI)

Bauman, Z (2001) *Community: seeking safety in an insecure world* Cambridge, Polity

Dekleva, B (1985) Raziskovanje odklonskih pojavov v zvezi z mladino *Revija za kriminalistiko in kriminologijo*, 4(36):295-303 Ljubljana, Inštitut za kriminologijo pri Pravni fakulteti

Dekleva, B, ed (1993) *Zivljenje v zavodu in potrebe otrok* (normalizacija) Ljubljana, Inštitut za kriminologijo pri Pravni fakulteti

Dekleva, B, Kobolt, A, and Klemenčič, M M (2006) Analysis of the achieved and needed competencies in the educational programme for social pedagogy at the Faculty of Education in Ljubljana In Tancig, S and Devjak, T, eds, *Contributions for Modernization of Educational Studies Programmes*, p150-169 Ljubljana, Pedagoška fakulteta

FICE Expert Seminar (1991) Neurimska deklaracija o izobraževanju socialnih pedagogo *FICE Edition*, 4:11-12 Hadasseh-Neurim Declaration on training child care workers

Garlichs, A and Leuzinger-Bohleber, M (1999) *Identität und Bindung Die Entwicklung von Beziehungen in Familie, Schule und Gesellschaft* Weinheim; München, Juventa-Verlag, Erziehung im Wandel; Band 2

Gottesmann, M, ed (1991) *Residential Child Care: An International Reader* London, Whiting and Birch, SCA Education series No 1

Gottesmann, M, ed (1994) *Recent Changes and New Trends in Extrafamilial Child Care: An International Perspective* London, Whiting and Birch

Jones, H D (1993) The training of social pedagogues in the European community after 1992. In Soisson, R, ed, *Politik, Forschung und Ausbildung in der Heimerziehung*, p153-159, Zürich, Fédération Internationale des Communautés Educatives, Collection of papers of FICE Congress

Klemenčič, M M, ed (2005) Modeli dobre prakse v socialnopedago_kem delu – strokovni izzivi v družbi negotovosti Združenje za socialno pedagogiko Ljubljana, Slovenska nacionalna sekcija FICE, zbornik povzetkov 3 slovenskega kongresa socialne pedagogike z mednarodno udeležbo, Rogla, 20-22 oktober 2005

Kobolt, A (1998) Identiteta in profesionalizacija stroke *Socialna pedagogika*, 2(1):422

Lorenz, W (1996) Social Professions for a Social Europe. In Seibel, F W and Lorenz, W, eds, *Soziale Professionen für ein Soziales Europa*, p39-50 Frankfurt/Main, IKO Verlag für Interkulturelle Kommunikation, ERASMUS-Evaluations-Konferenz, Koblenz 5-7.7.96

Ministrstvo za delo, dru_ino in socialne zadeve (2003) *Nacionalni razvojni program za izboljšanje položaja otrok v Republiki Sloveniji za obdobje 2003-2013* Ljubljana, Ministrstvo za delo, družino in socialne zadeve, Svet za otroke in Slovenski odbor za Unicef

Müller, B (1998) Siedler oder Trapper? Professionelles Handeln im pädagogischen Alltag der Offenen Jugendarbeit. In Deinet, U and Surzenhecker, B, eds, *Handbuch Offene Jugendarbeit*, p73-84 Münster, Votum

Peters, F and Wolff, M (1997) Handeln in (über-)komplexen Situationen Zur Professionalität in integrierten, flexiblen Hilfen *Forum Erziehungshilfen*, (3)

Schulz, G (1952-1966) Arten und Formen der Heime. In Trost, F, ed, *Handbuch der Heimerziehung*, p281-294 Frankfurt/Main; Berlin; Bonn; München, Diesterweg

Seibel, F W (1996) Internationale Kooperation Utopie oder vergessene Dimension? Szenische Darstellung auf der Basis der protokole der 1 und 2 Konferenz für Soziale Arbeit in Paris, 1928 bzw Frankfurt/Main 1932 In Seibel, F W and Lorenz, W, eds, *Soziale Professionen für ein Soziales Europa*, p15-38 Frankfurt/Main, IKO Verl für Interkulturelle Kommunikation, ERASMUS-Evaluations-Konferenz, Koblenz 5-7.7.96

Skalar, V (1988) Strokovni tokovi, ki so vplivajo na razvoj vzgojne in prevzgojne doktrine v vzgojnih zavodih *Ptički brez gnezda*, 13(6):27-43 Ljubljana: Društvo defektologov, Sekcija MVO

Sket, I (1993) Pregled raziskovalnega dela 1990-1993 Overview of research work 1990-1993 *Revija za kriminalistiko in kriminologijo*, 44

Thiersch, H and Rauschenbach, T (1987) Sozialpädagogik/Sozialarbeit: Theorie und Entwicklung In Eyferth, H et al, eds, *Handbuch zur Sozialarbeit, Sozialpädagogik* Neuwied; Darmstadt, Luchterhand, Studienausgabe edition

Trede, W (2001) Stationäre Erziehungshilfen im europäischen Vergleich. In Birtsch, V, Münstermann, K, and Trede, W, eds, *Handbuch Erziehungshilfen Leitfaden für Ausbildung*, Praxis und Forschung, p197-212 Münster, Votum

United Nations General Assembly (2002) S-27/2 *A world fit for children* Resolution adopted by the General Assembly

Vander Ven, K and Tittnich, E, eds (1986) *Competent Caregivers Competent Children: Training and Education for Child Care Practice* New York; London, Haworth

Vernooij, M A (1995) Training needs of teachers working with emotionally disturbed children. In Mittler, P and Duant, P, eds, *Teacher Education for Special Needs in Europe* London, Cassell

Winkler, M (1988) *Eine Theorie der Sozialpädagogik: über Erziehung als Rekonstruktion der Subjektivität* Stuttgart, Klett-Cotta, Konzepte der Humanwissenschaften

Winkler, M (2003) Theorie der Sozialpädagogik Annäherung mit Johann Nestroy. In Lauermann, K and Gerold, K, eds, *Sozialpädagogik in Österreich Perspektiven in Theorie und Praxis* Klagenfurt/ Celovec; Ljubljana/Laibach; Wien/Dunaj, Mohorjeva Hermagoras, Studien zur Sozialpädagogik Reihe des Instituts für Erziehungswissenschat und Bildungsforschung der Universität Klagenfurt

Zaviršek, D and Flaker, V (1995) Developing culturally sensitive services *Social work in Europe,* 2(2):30-36

Zorga, S (1997) Supervizija in profesionalni razvoj pedagoških delavcev. In Destovnik, K and Matovič, I, eds, *Izobraževanje učiteljev ob vstopu v tretje tisočletje: stanje, potrebe, rešitve* Ljubljana, Pedagoška fakulteta, zbornik prispevkov, Ljubljana, 6-7.6.97

8

The rehabilitation process for children and the role of the family

Kaija Klap

Child development and family relations
Attachment theory

One of the most crucial aspects of early development is the relationship between children and their primary caregivers. The quality of this experience of relationships is important in the later development of ideas about self and others. When the adult in charge of the child is personally and emotionally involved, a psychological interplay between adult and child will be superimposed on the events of bodily care. Such first attachments form the base from which further relationships develop.

Children bring to these relationships not only their needs for body comfort but also their emotional needs for affection, companionship and stimulating intimacy. When these needs are met reliably and regularly, the child-parent relationship becomes firm and benefits the children's intellectual and social development.

The central premise of attachment theory is that infants internalise the patterns of these early relationships with their attachment objects and build up a set of expectations about themselves in relation to others. On the basis of these first experiences they build what has been termed an 'Internal Working Model'. It means they can approach new situations with prior ideas about how they can cope in the face of threat. This model has three elements: the model of the self, the model of 'the other' and the model of the relationship between them.

Besides early attachment experiences, attachment theory emphasises the importance of substitute caring experiences. When planning extrafamilial placements the best interest of the child shall always be a primary consideration. Does the planned placement provide children with security, continuity in personal relations, care, understanding and love? Do the children have opportunities to feel closeness and share their thoughts and experiences? Is the overall picture of each child kept in mind?

Family as a system

Family therapist Virginia Satir sums up her perspectives about family life in four aspects that continually occur in troubled families:

- the feelings and ideas which individual family members have about themselves, in other words self-worth

- the ways family members communicate with one another

- the rules members of the family use for how they should feel and act, which eventually develop into family system

- the way members of the family relate to other people and institutions outside the family, how they link to society.

Satir describes the family as a closed or open system, depending upon how they react to change from outside. An open system offers choices and depends on successfully meeting reality for its continuing life. A closed system depends on edict and law and order and operates through force, both physically and psychologically.

> In the mobile all the pieces, no matter what size or shape, can be grouped together in balance by shortening or lengthening the strings attached, or rearranging the distance between the pieces. So it is with a family. None of the family members are identical to any other; they are all different and at different levels of growth. As in a mobile, you can't arrange one without thinking of the other. (Satir, 1978, p119).

Parenting
Parenting is a growth process

Therese Benedek's view of the parenting process helps us to understand generational family patterns (Anthony and Benedek, 1996). Every parent relives their own childhood in the process of parenting. The memories of being a child and of how they were parented are reactivated. Parents identify both with their parents and with their experience as children. Some parents become victims of their negative childhood experiences and repeat the past.

Some parents have certain strengths or environmental supports that help them to rework their pasts more positively as they raise their own children. By doing so they make parenting a developmental growth process. Good memories and positive experiences of how one was parented are resources in this growth process. Becoming a parent is a complicated process, influenced by the developmental phases of the family, social environment and cultural factors.

The basic skill in parenting is the ability to empathise. The feeling of empathy enables parents to identify with their children and understand their position and emotions. The ability to serve as a container means that the parent can receive and tolerate their own and the child's feelings without losing control. The parents' stability and the insight children receive from them help children to cope with their uncontrolled impulses. The ability to regress enables parents to enjoy playing with their children.

The ability of parents to keep up their role is the basis of a child's security. It means taking responsibility and authority in the child-parent relationship. Parents ought to have the capacity for creativeness instead of envy. Yet many parents and educators have difficulties in tolerating how children these days seem to have such an easy life. The alternative to envy is the ability to experience creativity and satisfaction in teaching, parenting and educating. From that point of view the child's success is a joy and rewarding experience. The ability for the child and parent to separate makes it possible for the child to grow through normal developmental crises. Some parents have certain skills but lack others. Some of them are able to respond to the needs of children at times but not with consistency.

Parental roles

Playing an adequate parental role in the child-parent relationship depends on the parent's ability to adjust to the changes in different developmental stages. As young couples become parents, they take on new roles. They have to meet the total dependency of a baby and then adapt to its growing individuality. In the early months of a baby's life the greatest demand on the parents is the need to meet this dependency.

The most important factors in the earlier years include the amount of time spent with the infant, the responsiveness to its physical needs and the ability to give priority to the child's needs over the parent's. Parents also need the capacity to invoke a sense of trust in the world around their children and the flexibility to grow with them so they know when an immediate response is required and when meeting the child's wishes is not urgent. Parents must be able to set firm limits and synchronise with a child's need to separate.

The later stage, after the age of four, is a time of ego consolidation. The child imitates, identifies and learns values and beliefs. Interpersonal relationships, attitudes towards achievement, morals and conscience formation and sexual identity are important developmental tasks.

Some parents are victims of their past experiences and repeat the generational pattern in their parenting. Anger and bitterness towards their families of origin disturb their relationships with their children. Sometimes parents want to correct this past experience by doing the opposite of what their own parents did, but this may not achieve their concept of good parenting and they may feel disappointed. To gain understanding of past experiences and to learn new ways of parenting, they need environmental support. Growing to be a parent is also an opportunity to recover and be freed from past experiences. The availability of social support greatly enhances the manageability of everyday life.

The parenting role is one part of an individual's personality. Stress experienced in other roles in an adult's life has an impact on parenting. In the backgrounds of some abusive parents there may be a history of early disturbance of attachment to their own parents, and this may influence the bonding process to their children (Gonzales-Ramos and Goldstein, 1989).

Complicated deliveries and illness during pregnancy may influence parent-infant attachment. Important parental factors in child maltreatment cases are the parents' lack of self-esteem and unresolved developmental needs. The parental role is a stressing and frustrating task to them. Parents may need their children to give them approval and meet their needs. There may be no empathy for a child as a separate person with individual needs and unique capacities. If the child fails to gratify the parental need or does not meet the parental expectations, then the parent's own infantile rage may be mobilised, resulting in physical abuse.

Alcohol and drug abuse are quite commonly linked to child maltreatment. Often parents who are at high risk of committing acts of abuse and neglect have been abused and neglected themselves, received poor parenting themselves, show low self-esteem, and are anxious, impulsive, apathetic, or lack knowledge about, and feel uncomfortable in, their parental roles.

Work with families

The basic principle in family work is accepting the uniqueness of each family. It certainly is not simple. Families we encounter in residential care often have a history of several crises. Even though families express their willingness to accept help they may not want to change long-standing habits, behaviours and ways of life. Richard Kagan and Shirley Schlosberg (1989) call family workers' attention to the conflicting agendas professionals and clients might have.

Most crisis-oriented families demonstrate a desire to reduce pain, to hide secrets that could threaten the family's balance, to remain loyal to the family, to get someone to control them and to utilise all possible resources and maintain a 'no change' position in defiance of outside controlling forces.

When the family lives from crisis to crisis, half the challenge for the family worker is how to remain in touch with the family, develop trust, and avoid the trap of becoming yet another helper who cannot help. Kagan and Schlosberg recognise that those working with families in perpetual crisis are in danger of becoming overwhelmed themselves. The process of engaging a family in making changes means sharing with the family the strengths, problems, feelings and dilemmas perceived and experienced by the worker.

In a situation where practitioners feel a greater urgency for change than the families themselves, it is not easy to develop positive strategies for building positive relationships with them. The crisis of the family can easily become the crisis of the family worker. The family worker may feel frustrated, anxious, helpless and hopeless. The client's feelings are absorbed by the family worker. Denying these feelings can lead to acting them out. The worker will look for someone to blame: the family, some family member, the referring authority, the supervisors, etc. Family workers may withdraw from, reject, or over-invest in clients, to overcome feelings of helplessness and hopelessness in the face of enormous unfulfilled needs. The worker's feelings, such as exhaustion, anticipation and dread, can be used as clues to the process in the family and the family's primary issues (Kagan and Schlosberg, 1989).

Work with crisis-oriented and chronically troubled families is very difficult and requires a clear perspective how these families function. It is important to maintain appropriate expectations for the work, and to define goals for the work and realise what kind of an outcome is regarded as a success. A family that can maintain itself, provide basic nurture and supervision for their children, and avoid abuse and neglect is a tremendous success story (Kagan and Schlosberg, 1989, p173). When the family members take responsibility for getting the assistance they need, it should be seen as a sign of positive outcome.

In extrafamilial care our basic task is to care for and facilitate and promote the growth of the children. Giving priority to this task should guide family workers in the process of assessing the collaborative role of the child's family and other people close to him /her.

A residential care unit's supports are crucial to equipping workers with the knowledge, skills, and help essential to keeping up goal-oriented working roles and to combating staff turnover and burnout. Structured time for supervision is needed. The supervisor can help to understand and look at what is going on in the cycle of interaction involving the family, the family worker and other people involved in the process. The supervisor can help to identify the pain in the family, the patterns of interaction, the underlying meaning of events, and how to maintain the family's balance in a crisis. Without regular supervision sensitive family workers will react more to the stressing feelings than to the ongoing dynamics. When the feelings become predominant over attempts to hypothesise and understand, the worker loses the ability to be helpful in the situation.

Work with families begins from where they are. A one-model approach with strict rules does not recognise family members' special needs and strengths. Often it takes time to involve all family members, sometimes with no success. Even so, the family worker must keep in mind the larger multigenerational family and ecosystem and keep explaining as often as necessary that the placement is a helping plan and not synonymous with abandonment or punishment.

The family worker may succeed in involving the whole family and it may look as if working together is going well. The stressful feelings in the family may be sensed by the worker but not dealt with for fear of losing the family and being abandoned. Working for change includes confronting the problems. Being an accepted supporter of the family system is not enough, especially in cases where a child or other family member is suffering.

When working with multi-problem families, miraculous cures cannot be expected. Changes for the better are small. Many families could list a number of professionals who have tried to help them but failed. The family may mention these workers and the current family worker may be tempted to discount past workers. It is helpful to learn about past treatment experiences and there is no place for workers with egocentric attitudes who are only prepared to see things from their own viewpoint. Being realistic as a worker involves persisting in maintaining realistic expectations and acknowledging the small changes.

Work with troubled families means developing positive connections. This is impossible if the staff see nothing positive in the family. To like or dislike a family is a judgement. A worker's feelings and reactions may provides clues to family dynamics but it is important to avoid becoming judgemental. Sometimes positive connections can be found through organising different kind of opportunities to reach out to the family. In Lauste Family Rehabilitation Centre (www.lauste.fi) we try to show our respect by hospitality, which means providing opportunities to participate in family camps and providing bed and board any time the family wants to visit the Centre.

Rehabilitative extrafamilial care
Setting goals

Rehabilitation refers to something that has to be healed or get better. In extrafamilial care children and their family relations have broken down or the network of close relationships never developed to meet children's age-appropriate developmental needs. A child's life is a continuum of past, present and future, so it is important to redirect treatment efforts so that children and young people facing emotional obstacles to independence receive the special assistance they need. They need special assistance on the following matters:

- how to resolve the issues of maltreatment, abuse and separation

- how to form at least one close relationship

- how to improve their lost self-esteem and mature emotionally and socially

- how to make peace with the family.

After a long lasting collaborative relationship with the family and the child the issues mentioned above can be dealt with.

The family as a partner in the child's treatment and upbringing process

The practices used in Lauste Family Rehabilitation Centre illustrate how we try to help the children and youngsters to solve situations such as those I have described. Lauste Family Rehabilitation centre is a private institution providing residential care, a special school and after-care services to boys and girls from the age of 12 to 21.

- ▨ In Lauste Family Rehabilitation Centre family work is an integral part of child's treatment and upbringing process.

- ▨ The focus in family work is on the child. The goal of collaboration with parents is to secure the child's well-being and development.

- ▨ Staff members doing family work and parents are in complementary role to one another.

As a result of these principles parents have become important participants in the treatment and upbringing process, and in evaluating children's behaviour staff keep in mind family history and relations.

The treatment and upbringing process has been influenced by principles of structural family therapy theory. In family work and in educational work in group homes the importance of age-appropriate role is emphasised. That means that power, responsibility and care given to the child match the child's developmental stage. This attitude has an impact on family work. Respecting the family means emphasising its position and significance in various collaborative settings and in the process of assessing children's individual development and attachment.

Separation and loss

When children are living in residential care, loss and separation are key issues for them as well as for their parents. The impact of separation can be equally severe whatever the reason for it. Children feel the pain that separations bring. They feel abandoned, unloved and lonely, and their ability to trust is threatened.

Most of the placements to Lauste Family Rehabilitation Centre have been carried out in cooperation with the parents or the placement is officially arranged with the parents' consent. In the beginning of the placements it is important to relieve the emotional crisis which both parents and child experience because of the separation. Often parents feel guilty and cannot accept the placement readily. There is an empty place around the dinner table. Sometimes the child's reaction to the placement is strong and it provokes doubts and questions in parents, eg Are the staff qualified enough to handle the situation? Does the child accuse them because of the placement?

The team in the group home is prepared to listen to the child and the parents. The child's own educator especially has an active role in keeping parents informed about the child's life in the group home. The educator also consults the parents about the behaviour, habits and other practical everyday matters.

The parents are told about their child's well-being and about conflicts with the staff and other children.

Often the content of discussions with the parents is related to the process before the placement. Why did this process start, who is guilty, is the child accusing them? The parents need support to be able to meet the child for the first time after the placement. The child's behaviour toward them can sometimes be demanding, accusing and threatening. Often children drive a hard bargain with the parents. 'Take me out from here or I'll run away'. 'Bring cigarettes or money or...' . Sometimes parents obey and thus create a secret that gives the power to the child.

Some parents cannot face their children after the placement. They cannot endure the feelings activated by the process. They do not answer the phone. They do not contact the child or the staff. Parents suffering from chemical dependency become worse. Sometimes the family makes new arrangements at home; children who are in Lauste may lose their rooms to siblings, for example, or their belongings may be put away out of sight.

Listening empathetically to the feelings experienced by the family and the child is the means to help them to recover. The staff in the group home concentrate on helping children through this stage and the social worker takes responsibility for listening to the parents to build the trust that is so vital in collaborative work.

Forming an alliance with the family

It is characteristic of parents whose children are in care to feel helpless and powerless. They perceive themselves as victims of the system that controls them and feel that they have no power over the decisions others are making about their lives and the lives of their children. Such reactions can inhibit progress in a number of ways. When parents feel that their actions have no impact, it is easy to give up. Unless they believe that they have some power in the decision-making, it is unlikely that they will mobilise themselves to make changes. If one has no power in a situation one cannot be held accountable. Workers have a responsibility to acknowledge the feelings parents have and help them regain some control and power, and the parents need to know that their participation in the treatment and upbringing process is vital.

In the beginning of the family work process, the goal is to build trust that makes possible the collaborative relationship between the staff and parents. A collaborative relationship entails commitment to participation in the child's treatment and upbringing. A written agreement on goals and tasks gives parents a strong feeling of participation. When both parties in the collaborative relationship need one another, it is a sign of a well-functioning relationship. Building a successful collaborative relationship with the parents depends on the staff's ability to empathise with parents' experiences so that parents can sense it. The experience of being heard encourages the parents to participate and to feel that their involvement is important. Trust is built through interaction. This trust is needed to deal with hurt, shame and anger and to find shared explanations and meanings of emotions, behaviours and events.

Careworkers in residential care have to accept parenting functions being part of their role. Parents are well informed of the principles behind the everyday practices. They are asked for collaboration in their children's upbringing. This collaborative position is one of the most important parts in family work throughout the placement.

Parents and siblings are invited to visit the institution and are encouraged to keep active contact with the children in care. Siblings participate in family sessions and their reactions and feelings are dealt with. The whole family has an important role and meaning in the helping process. Children in care need to experience their family's presence and their parents' participation in decision-making concerning their life.

Shared parenting

Shared parenting is an often used concept in the field of child welfare. What it means in practice depends on the goals expressed in a child's individual care plan. Placements in the long term set different kind of demands for shared parenting than short-term placements. The roles in this kind of a collaborative relationship must be clear and the tasks should be written in the service agreement.

Parents of children in extrafamilial care tend to remember their children as they were at the time of the placement if they have no opportunities to stay in touch with their children as they grow.

Regular meetings which structure the work
Pre-placement visit

Before being placed at Lauste, children visit the Family Rehabilitation Centre together with the parents and the referring social worker. Participants from the Lauste Rehabilitation Centre in this visiting meeting are the social therapist, the teacher and the educator from the group home. The purpose of

In the view of the child in care	In the view of the parent	In the view of the staff
Experience of parents' interest and involvement	Experience of involvement in care and upbringing of the child	Adopting an adequate role in collaborative relationship to meet the needs of the child and the family
Experience of collaboration between parents and staff	Staying in touch with the growth and development of the child	Listening to parents' thoughts and bringing them up in discussions
Experience of continuity	Seeing new possibilities and analysing past events	Dealing with and understanding the child's history and raising issues about future possibilities
Experience of the parents having a respected and meaningful role and authority	Getting and giving support in difficulties	Getting and giving support as well as acknowledging the parents' resources
Being up to date with parents' expectations and thoughts	Staying aware of the child's wishes and expectations as well as with the staff's views	Supporting the interaction between the child and the parents as well as facilitating discussion
Awareness of parents' involvement	Awareness of everyday life and the principles behind the practices	Maintaining an open and confidential atmosphere

Table 1: The functions of shared parenting

the meeting is to listen to the views of the child, the parents and the referring social worker about the placement The services and principles of the Rehabilitation Centre and special school are introduced. This information is given to the family in writing also. The family's active participation during the placement is emphasised.

The first care conference

The care plan is the basic record drawn up by municipal child welfare services together with the client. It is a legal document expressing how in each individual case the best interest of the child should be implemented. The Child Welfare Act seeks to promote continuity in the child's life, underlining the right to be in contact with people close to the child.

The care plan is a long-term document (eg to secure children's healthy development) which is transformed into individual goals through the collaborative working process that includes the parents, the children's networks and staff working in extrafamilial care.

A service agreement establishes the goals to be achieved during the placement. The child, the family, the referring social worker and the educator, the social therapist and the teacher from Family Rehabilitation Centre are involved in the preparation of the agreement. All the parties involved get the written copy of the agreement, which is written in the early phase of the placement. The service agreement serves a variety of purposes including:

- maintaining a focus on the child's needs
- ensuring clarity of tasks and goals for the child, the family, the referring social worker and the staff in the Family Rehabilitation Centre
- facilitating decision-making on the part of the parents, social worker, child and Family Rehabilitation Centre
- specifying time frames for decision-making
- encouraging the participation of the parents and thereby promoting their sense of competence and control
- providing for periodic review and assessment of progress.

In the first care conference practical plans are made concerning family contact with the child and how the staff in the group home keep in touch with the family.

At the beginning of the placement the child does not spend weekends at home. The family is welcome to visit the centre and stay overnight in a guest room. The first weeks are for the child to settle into the new environment, learning the house rules, getting acquainted with his/her own educator and other team members, other children living in the group home and attending school.

After that phase the child is allowed to spend weekends at home. The family and child's own educator set behaviour rules that the child is expected to follow during his/her stay at home. Breaking the rules has a consequence: the child spends the following weekend in the group home. These situations are opportunities to support the parents' authority and share their worries and ideas among the parents and child care workers. It is not always easy to reach mutual understanding of the rules. Parents do not want to make the child angry and because of that they avoid the responsibility for decision-making.

The forms of the family work depend on the assessment made of the need for change. Lauste Family Rehabilitation Centre has a structured working model, which is necessary for maintaining the practices of periodic review and assessment of progress.

The child's situation in the Family Rehabilitation Centre and special school is regularly reviewed by the team consisting of the child's own educator, the teacher and the social therapist. This team and the child meet regularly to review how the child is achieving his/her goals, how the team has helped with this task and what should be done differently. This meeting has a function to prepare the child for the care conference where his/her parents and referring social worker are present.

The child needs to know and experience in practice:

- who the adults are who are involved in decision-making and in caring for him

- what the expectations are which he is supposed to meet and how he is thought of

- what kind of collaboration with adults is helpful for him

- how, where and by whom his thoughts and wishes are listened to.

In the care conference parents and the referring social worker get feedback of child's achievements and problems and they give feedback to the child and the care team. All parties contribute their opinions about child's development and goals that need to be worked for. The relations between the care team, the parents and the referring social worker are also evaluated.

The feedback given to children must be clear and based on facts, encouraging and motivating, and take into consideration their individual capabilities. Feedback is not only for analysing weaknesses and strengths. It also includes the idea that skills and good qualities become strengths after they have been acknowledged by the people meaningful to the children. Gaining strengths means heightening children's self-esteem.

The family's needs for support and concrete plans for collaboration are discussed in the care conference. A written report of the discussions is given to those involved in the treatment and upbringing process.

Family work and working methods

The focus of family work is on the child or the youngster. We want the attitudes that guide the practical work to be openness, mutual advice and help. The parents and the care team share responsibility for the upbringing and treatment process.

Special considerations pertinent to family work in extrafamilial care emerge in the following areas:

- family history
- functioning of family and parents
- psychological, psychiatric, and medical evaluations of parents
- parents' response to children in different developmental stages
- recognition of parents' strengths
- appreciation of the family's environment.

In addition to the areas mentioned above the characteristics of abusive and neglectful parents must be considered. Most children in care have experienced parental abuse or neglect.

Tools for assessing the functioning of families and facilitating the treatment process include:

- timeline
- genogram
- ecomap
- various family therapy techniques: problem-solving, giving directives etc.
- various interviewing techniques.

Observation of the family's current functioning is an integral part of the assessment process. A home visit provides an opportunity to evaluate the basic living conditions of the family. The ecological perspective on social work practice requires that a person's functioning and characteristics are not viewed in isolation from the environment. Accordingly the working area and technique used take account of each family and child's unique situation and the stage of the treatment process.

Work methods and the timing for dealing with various problems in the family depend on how they affect the child's life at the moment. Changes in the family's internal and external environments may require involving consultative resources. Divorcing families are often in the state of disorganisation where relationships with the extended family, friends and neighbours, work, school and health services are unsettled.

Families and children in residential care are likely to raise powerful and primitive feelings and fantasies in staff who suffer painful though sometimes unacknowledged identifications with clients, and who have intense reactions to them, both positive and negative, such as pity for their plight and fear about their violence. Staff need adequate support to work through the feelings they have experienced with troubled clients. Feelings that cannot be worked with tend to become to be built into the structure, culture and mode of functioning of the institution and thereby impair task-performance.

Lauste Family Rehabilitation Centre use a regular structure for reflecting experiences and observations in relation to clients which entails:

- immediate discussions with the colleagues
- team meetings every three weeks
- supervision on a regular basis
- consultation with specialists whenever needed
- care meetings (establishing and evaluating goals and tasks).

Family work is implemented in various settings. Families are invited to participate in recreational activities along with staff, children and other parents. Children and staff usually plan the programme with the interests of the siblings in mind. Children living in the group home have an opportunity to give pleasure to their families. Every year group homes in the Lauste Family Rehabilitation Centre organise an 'open doors day'. The parents of the children are invited to spend a day in the group home and also meet other families. The school organises traditional celebrations at the end of the semester and before Christmas. Most families participate in these occasions.

The children's own educators and social therapists work together with the families. In the course of the family work process they gain understanding of the realities of the children's life. This understanding is needed for treating each child. The children's thoughts and feelings about themselves as members of their families are brought into focus. The children's own educators have a specific role in bringing their observations and experiences of the children's behaviour and motives to the family meetings where they are explored together with the children and their families, to help resolve inconsistencies between the explanation given by the children's families and those of the staff. An important aspect in dealing with parent-child relationships is to understand how children influence their parents' concept of themselves and vice versa. There are various work books and other materials that can be used as facilitative tools for such assessments.

The role of the children's educators in supporting children and their families

Each child has their own educator in the group home, who participates in all the meetings during the treatment process. In the initial phase, educators are actively in contact with the parents. They participate in:

- care conferences
- family work process
- care meetings with the teacher, social therapist and child
- network meetings (child's health services, other authorities etc.).

Educators have the role of advocate. They are responsible for informing the other team members, teacher and social therapist about the child's situation. They are also responsible for checking that decisions concerning the child are carried out as planned. Each child's educator initiates discussions with the staff and follows the child's behaviour and development at school, in group home, various cultural and sports groups closely. The child's own educator is a partner in parenting.

Educators may use the following approaches in their relationship with the child:

- Writing about painful issues in a diary – such correspondence has been found to be a fruitful non-threatening way of communicating, especially with girls.

- Regular individual sessions together, whether for discussion or going to a movie, shopping etc. Many children in care do not know how to love themselves, and they need to be taught how to care for themselves and find healthy enjoyment.

- Work books focusing on areas of the children's lives, such as social skills, sexuality, family relations and values. They are helpful in assessing children's skills and problematic attitudes towards themselves and to others, or to alcohol and drugs. Memories of the time in the group home may be meaningful to the children later in life.

The child's own educator plays a central role in the child's life during the placement. The relationships staff develop with the children determine the success or failure of interventions. There are many professionals in different roles working with the child and they must all commit themselves to tolerating stormy periods in order to maintain a strong supportive relationship with the child.

Close relations and getting on well in life

What are the crucial factors that make a difference in the lives of children who have had difficult backgrounds? Some grow into healthy adults and parents who are capable of meeting their own children's needs, whereas others face great difficulties as they grow up.

Studies show how protective factors such as social networks and close relationships have a positive impact on getting children's future lives. Such protective factors might be in the child's environment outside the family. Achievements and success in some areas of life can compensate for stressful experiences in the family. Positive experiences in areas that are valued by children heighten their self-esteem. Experience of overcoming crises gives children resources to face troubles later in life. According to studies, the most important factors influencing development are the children's cognitive explanations to themselves about events and experiences in their lives and their ability to share them (Halmemies, 1998).

Young adults who had grown up in extrafamilial care from early childhood were the subject of a study that classified them into three typical categories in accordance with how they coped. The categories were: those who get along well, the survivors and the embittered. Those who get along well had had an attachment figure replacing the parent during their placement, whereas the other two groups did not. Those who get along well had had close long-lasting friendships outside the substitute care place, whereas the others had contacts only with the peers living in the same place (Halmemies, 1998).

Children in care and their families have often lost their social networks because of unresolved conflicts in their relations and frequent moving. Unresolved conflicts affect children's relationships. Parents may disagree about whom the child may see and who has the power to control them. Children can be trapped between fighting adults. The goal in family work is to untie knots that prevent children from having connection with those to whom they feel close. Children's networks are made up of connections with siblings, aunts, grandparents, cousins and friends, and they influence their identity. Often children in care do not know where they belong or who is missing them.

In the care system we need to keep in mind from the very beginning of the placement that some day children will leave care. Where will they go then and who will be part of their life after leaving care? It is not always possible to return home.

Children living in troubled families do not have high expectations of the future. They fear that they may not be able to avoid the problems their parents had: alcoholism, sickness, poverty, unemployment, violence etc. Families do not have the means to encourage or help them to choose differently. Again, children may feel guilty about having better chances than their parents had. Children need help to understand that even though parents cannot change their situation for the better, they wish their children a good life. When parents and staff members work side by side for the best for children, parents can be proud of their achievements. If they have participated in their children's treatment and upbringing, they have supported their positive development.

Ending the placement

The placements in Lauste Family Rehabilitation centre last approximately about one and a half to two years. Almost all placements are planned to see children through their comprehensive schooling. During the last school year the main goal is to plan and determine where children will live and which school they will attend. In this phase the importance of the support of the children's networks increases. Who are the people committed to be part of their life after they leave care? This is the most important question of all.

The plan for the new phase in the children's lives must be tailored to individual needs. Most youngsters leaving residential care need to learn many skills if they are to build their new living environment, maintain themselves and develop themselves further. They will face practical, cognitive, social, and emotional tasks in their the new living environment. The construction of a supportive network depends on their needs and abilities. The plan of action is drawn up together with the children, their family, the municipal social worker and the care team at the Centre.

Multi-professional team approach

The dynamics in a community like Lauste Family Rehabilitation Centre are complicated. Complications arise from the fact that the staff have many roles in different processes. The concrete task and role in relation to family, child, team and municipal social services require awareness of the entire treatment and upbringing process. It is equally important to understand also the tasks and roles of other people who participate in the process. Collaborative work succeeds only when the participants involved in the process see one another in complementary roles. In addition to mutual understanding of roles there must be a framework that makes continuity and regularity possible. The established procedure includes meetings and mutual understanding of the principles that guide the work in the treatment and upbringing process.

The multi-professional team approach in assessment and treatment planning

T A S K S

social therapist	child's own educator	teacher	team in group home
-lifeline based on records -keeps in touch with the family and network -participates in weekly evaluation sessions at school -monitors daily report -consults psychiatrist as necessary -organises the meetings and coordinates the collaborative work	-substance abuse assessment scale -ecomap -timeline -follows daily report -keeps in touch with the family -participates weekly in evaluation sessions at school - makes a summary of daily reports and brings it to the team meeting	-evaluations of academic and social skills and behaviour -assessment of child's learning problems -daily contact with the group home	-every team member writes daily report on child's behaviour, mood swings, skills, contacts with the family etc. -helps the child to settle down

team meeting once every three weeks
social therapist, the team of the group home

PARTICIPANTS IN THE CARE MEETING:
the child, teacher, child's own educator, social therapist

1. Observations and experiences of the child are discussed to determine the guidelines in treatment and upbringing process. The team reflects on behaviour in relation to the child's past experiences and relations.
2. The time line based on the information in official records is compared with the one based on the information given by the child. The team makes an initial estimate of how to deal with the past in individual and family work.
3. Risks and protective factors in child's life are mapped. Initial assessment of the working methods.
4. The assessment of intoxicant abuse is relieved and determined the action needed in the situation
5. Questions and observations coming up during the meeting are written down and brought up in discussions with the child and the family.

Care meeting
1. Listening to child's wishes and experiences.
2. Giving feedback to the child about his/her behaviour and achievements in the group home and the school.
3. Child's feelings and thoughts concerning the placement are discussed.
4. Discussion of the goals and an estimate of how long the placement is planned to last.
5. The child is prepared for the care conference, which the parents and the referring social worker are also attending

case conference; goal oriented plans, checking the progress

network participants; parents, social worker

Assessment refers to collecting and analysing information and formulating goals. Goals must be concrete, attainable, and open to evaluation. Besides description of the goals, the plan explains how, when, and by whom the goals are going to be realised. The treatment plan is reviewed regularly and emphasis is placed on the description of the progress.

Increasing social competence

One of the most important tasks in residential care is to help children overcome or reduce developmental lags. For children to learn skills they must be given tasks that link up with their capabilities and offer sufficient challenge and learning opportunities for further development.

The learning and teaching environment in Lauste Family Rehabilitation Centre has the following elements:

- physical environment, daily routines, house rules
- special school
- the educators' predictable, systematic action in everyday life
- feedback systems, structured working models
- assessment and treatment planning
- supplementary treatment by specialists (therapists etc).

Competence can be conceived as having sufficient skills to fulfil the tasks one meets in everyday life. Competence is influenced by factors such as circumstances in the family, the loss of a loved one, neglect, physical health and so on. Children in residential care have severe behaviour problems. In social situations their behaviour leads to negative consequences. They have trouble achieving their goals. When children become accepted in the peer group and joint activities, they have both sufficient co-operation skills and ability to communicate and empathise with other children's feelings as well as appropriate ways of expressing their own feelings, such as aggression.

The skill to establish and maintain relationships is the result of a long interactional process. It is recognised that child-rearing experiences, particularly in the early years, also affect the capacity of children to regulate their aggressive impulses. Some young people are raised by parents with severe personality problems, and these hinder the psychological structures that children develop to adapt to their environment. When working with children and families with such difficulties we must believe that the children with developmental damage have the capacity to grow.

Summary

Despite disappointments and hurt, children's families are their lifeline. Children and youngsters identify with their parents and are protective of their families. They are also angry with their families. It takes a long time before child become ready to acknowledge the family's strengths and weaknesses. They need help to move toward independence without feeling guilty about being more successful than their families.

Children need to address emotional issues related to past experiences suffered, to their feelings, to their identity and their interpersonal relationships with others. To accomplish these tasks they need the support and commitment of trained staff. Young people need a sense of self-worth before they have the confidence they need to take full responsibility for their lives. In residential care we have to help the children clarify their goals step by step, and serve as role models for achieving their aspirations.

References

Anthony, E J and Benedek, T, eds (1996) *Parenthood: its psychology and psychopathy* London, Aronson

Gonzalez-Ramos, G and Goldstein, E G (1989) Child maltreatment: an overview. In Ehrenkranz, S M, Goldstein, E G, Goodman, L, and Seinfeld, J, eds, *Clinical social work with maltreated children and their families: an introduction to practice*, Chapter 1, p3-20 London, New York University Press

Halmemies, S (1998) Lastensuojeluperheen lapsen kokemukset *Tieto kiertoon – monistesarja*, (11)

Kagan, R and Schlosberg, S (1989) *Families in perpetual crisis* London, Norton

Satir, V (1978) *Peoplemaking* London, Souvenir

9

Preserving and rehabilitating family relationships in residential group care

Emmanuel Grupper and Irit Mero-Jaffe

Introduction

For some years now, in Israel and throughout the professional world, there has been an increasing awareness among those who work in the field of residential care that it is essential to change the attitude of professional staff with regard to the families of children in residential group care (Wiener, 1990; Poso, 1996; Grupper, 1998; Garfat and McElwee, 2004). To do this, the families must be encouraged to take an active part in their children's lives while they are growing up in group care. By involving the parents in the life of the group home, it may be possible for professional staff to empower the parents and help them rehabilitate the relationship between them and their children (Buhler-Niederberger, 1999). This will add an important new dimension to the treatment offered to the child by the group home. A significant gap exists, even nowadays, between the verbally expressed professional attitude towards strengthening the children's relationships with their parents and the implementation of these expressions in the field.

There are, however, interesting examples of locally initiated programmes that aim to strengthen parent-child relationships within various group homes in Israel and elsewhere (Guttman, 2001).

Yeladim – the Council for the Child in Placement, a voluntary non-profit organisation working with Israeli children in group care programmes, has learned from experience with several residential group homes in Israel that family relationship programmes can be successfully implemented. Com-

ponents of these local initiatives have been integrated into an overall programme proposal called Preservation and Rehabilitation of Family Relationships. With the backing and financial support of Israel's Social Security
Special Projects Fund since the 2002-2003 academic year, this overall programme has been operating in four selected group homes for children at risk,
removed from their families by the Social Welfare Services. This has been a
three year pilot project, and one of its goals is to bring about a change in the
staff's attitude in the four participating group homes towards parents. The
information accumulated from the project about how such a change can be
brought about and how to work with parents should be consolidated in a
form that will be useful for the entire residential group care system.

This chapter is based on a systematic evaluation of that programme, undertaken by the two authors.

Theoretical framework

For many decades it was largely accepted that residential programmes are
intended to 'save the children from their families' (Wiener, 1990). Anita
Wiener claims that this kind of policy was aiming at giving children a new
chance in a place that both separated them from the negative influence of
their natural environment in the family and the neighbourhood, and also exposed them to powerful and enriching environments in residential programmes.

The result was that parents were completely ignored, being considered as
'part of the problem' and not as potential partners for 'solving the children's
problems' (Pasternak, 1994). Balster (1991) and Sarason (1996) refer to the
same problem in the school system, which nowadays understands the importance of involving parents in the educational process. This is particularly
important with youth at risk, because it has the potential to reduce their feelings of alienation towards educators. Laufer (1991) emphasises that every
residential programme exposes the child to a particular 'cultural scene', in
Eisikovits's terms (1980), which is rather different from the cultural background at home.

So it is of utmost importance to bridge the gap between these two worlds. It
might help children to adjust to residential care life (Kashty *et al*, 2000). And
programmes that seek to work with parents trying to empower them as
parents will also facilitate the children's possibilities to find their place in the
family after they leave residential care. These outcomes can be achieved only
when educators seek to strengthen their contacts with parents. In Great

Britain, this educational policy is underlined by a special law, namely the Children Act 1989. It states clearly that parents must be involved in their children's education even when the children are in care, and caregivers are obliged to work in collaboration with parents and encourage them to increase their involvement (Kahan, 1992).

The same has been happening recently in Israel. An official report regarding children's rights in extra-familial care indicates that:

> There is a wish for a collaborative work of welfare authorities with the parents...The parent's participation is derived out of their responsibility, duty and rights as parents in order to guarantee the child's best interest...However, not all professionals are willing to adopt the attitude of partnership in their everyday practice. Therefore, the new law proposal (paragraph 56), is defining this responsibility very clearly, in the way to impose a full implementation of these principles... (Rot Levy, 2003, p246)

However, the transition from the past attitude towards parents to the 'partnership policy' is not easy. Garfat and McElwee (2004) claim that it is easier to create an atmosphere of collaboration with parents while the staff members are new workers who have not worked in residential care settings which display negative attitudes towards parents. The process of changing the habits and attitudes of professionals already in post can be difficult and complicated. This is exactly the challenge of the project evaluated here, a project that aims to change the attitudes towards parents with experienced staff members in four treatment-oriented residential programmes in Israel.

The programme's objectives

Three objectives were established when the programme was launched:

- to help blunt the parent-child conflicts inherent in the dual loyalties faced by children towards their parents and towards the residential group homes' staff members
- to improve the relationship between children and their parents as well as with the group home staff
- to improve the self-image of the parents and increase their ability to function as parents.

These objectives led to the following overall aims, defined for each of the partners involved:

Objectives for children in residential care
- to improve the child's adjustment to the group home and her/his behaviour

123

- to strengthen the child's relationships with her/his family
- to improve the child's self-image.

Objectives for parents

- to increase parents' trust in residential staff and strengthen their collaboration with staff members
- to raise parents' awareness of their children's needs and of their actual and potential strengths
- to increase the parents' willingness to participate in their children's education, even though they are not living at home and thus improve their parental competences.

Objectives for residential staff

- to increase the professional staff's understanding of children and their families in order to advance the children's education and development
- to make parents full partners in the children's educational process and empower their parental competences
- to view the parents as if they were additional clients of the group home.

Some of these goals and aims are similar to those of programmes in other residential care networks throughout the world (Dolev *et al*, 1997).

The design of the intervention programme

Three components that bear in themselves the potential to integrate parents into the lives of children in residential group care were included in the Programme. The experimental phase consisting of these was originally planned for two consecutive years and entailed:

1   Ongoing dynamic workshops for parents in the group home, on a by-weekly basis, throughout the course of the year. Every visit of the parents was composed of three parts: First, a structured dynamic group activity for parents among themselves (groups for mothers and groups for fathers). Second, structured group activities for parents together with their children. After that, parents were allowed to engage in free activities with their children as they wished, either on the campus of the group home, such as having a quiet walk together, or preparing dinner in the dormitory, or perhaps going out to buy an ice-cream in the neighbourhood.

2   All members of the children's families were invited to family days at the group home, three or four times a year. The group home staff organised transport. Participation in the group sessions was open only to parents selected for it. Well in advance, parents received a well designed invitation card with a detailed time-table of all activities. Children were highly involved in the preparation of family day activities. They prepared shows such as singing and dancing and also activities that were deliberately designed so they had to be done together by parents and their children.

3   Child-parent intensive summer camp for mothers (5-6 days) or fathers (3-4 days) together with their children. Parents slept in the same room as their children and shared the many common activities in swimming pools, on trips, or in play that required active collaboration between parents and their children. Most important was how this provided a unique experience for children to have their mother's or father's undivided attention over several days.

Although some of these components had been included in the programmes of various group homes, there had never been an overall programme that integrated these elements in a structured and simultaneous way. The assumption was that such integration increases the likelihood of significant positive results.

The evaluation and research methodology

The pilot project continued for three years but, as a result of budget constraints, the evaluation covered only the first two years of the three year pilot project. We were designated as the research evaluation team, as we are part of the Educational Research and Evaluation Unit of Beit Berl University College, and we are grateful to the Israeli Social Security Special Projects Fund for the authorisation to use the research material for this chapter.

The evaluation research methodology was based on a combination of qualitative and quantitative research instruments, namely, open-ended observations, semi-structured or open-ended interviews, gathering documents and artifacts together with quantitative instruments that included the workshop group leaders (the treatment staff), residential direct care workers (the educational staff), and the staff's supervisors filling out various questionnaires. This integration of quantitative and qualitative methods in research is becoming common (Taylor, 2000). The methods are regarded as complementary and not as substituting one another. The large amount of raw material that was collected during the research field work was analysed qualitatively through content analysis, together with a quantitative statistical analysis of the questionnaire data using T scale for significant variance between groups, and the Scheffee test for analysis of more subtle factors (Beyth-Marom, 1988).

The raw material was the outcome of the following fieldwork activities undertaken during the two year evaluation period (see also Appendix Table 1, for details of these research tools).

Analysing documents: the kind of documents analysed were: protocols of meetings, documents prepared by local staff members, letters written by children or parents, invitation cards to the parents' day, programmes of summer camp activities, etc (55 documents altogether over 2 years).

Semi-structured interviews: these included the directors of the four group homes, the national coordinator of the programme and the local coordinator in all four residential programmes, together with all seventeen social workers who were leading the group activities with parents. Interviews were done twice, at the beginning of every school year and again at the end (a total of 51 interviews over 2 years).

Occasional interviews: these were done through the year with the workers leading the group activities, before or directly after a session, with parents, children and other workers of the group home (119 interviews over 2 years).

Open-ended observations: the only activity where we could not make direct observations because of ethical problems were the dynamic group sessions of the parents by themselves. In all other activities participant observations were made by the research team: in group activities for parents with children, in free activity of children with parents, in family days, and in the different activities of the summer camps for parents and children (54 observations over 2 years).

Questionnaires: in order to close the gap of information about the dynamic group activities, group leaders filled in a structured questionnaire after every group activity. The supervisors of these group leaders were asked to complete questionnaires too, and the residential group care workers (the educational staff) filled questionnaires about the free activities of parents with their children in the dormitories. These questionnaires contained open-ended questions that were analysed by use of qualitative methods (798 questionnaires altogether).

Because of all the research tools used, the researchers obtained a wide range of field material that is of great importance for evaluating such a programme from different perspectives.

The figures about parents' active participation in the dynamic group sessions in the four residential group homes (A, B, C, D), is presented in the following table:

| Group home | School year 2002-2003 | | | School year 2003-2004 | | | Total | |
	fathers	mothers I	mothers II	fathers	mothers I	mothers II	2002-2003	2003-2004
A	5	4	4	5	4	4	13	13
B	8	1	4	6	10	7	22	23
C	9	11	10	6	9	12	30	24
D	0	10	8	0	6	8	18	14
Total	22	35	26	17	29	31	83	74

Parents' Active Participation in Dynamic Group Sessions

The same eleven dynamic groups that functioned in the first year continued to function in the second year, although some participants changed. Some parents left the group at the end of the first year and others joined. It was a challenge for both the participants and group leaders to continue the group process with a newly composed parents' group. These workshops were based on a co-leading group work model, involving twenty-two group leaders.

Results and findings

In order to evaluate the influence of the programme on parents' relationships with group home staff, a six-parameter criterion was defined, consisting of:

- Parent increases number of visits to the group home (not counting visits for participating in the workshops)
- Parent phone calls to staff members or child increase
- Parent shows interest in being more involved in the activities of the group home
- Parent participates regularly in workshops
- Parent is more willing to share problems with staff members
- Parent is more satisfied with the group home generally

The partners – group leaders, group care workers and parents – were all asked the same questions and the answers of all three groups tended to be similar. Qualitative material gathered in interviews, and participant observations augmented this result, but a statistical difference was found and the reason for this, revealed by the Scheffee test, was the increased enthusiasm expressed by the parents.

The question relating to the empowerment of parents and improving their self esteem and parental competences was checked by asking the professionals. Group leaders thought that parents had changed significantly but the residential group care workers thought that the changes were slight. Another question probed the relationships between parents and their children, exploring:

■ whether parents become more interested in what was happening with their child

■ whether children were entitled to visit home more frequently than before

■ whether children report better relationships with parents during visits at home

■ whether the separation of parents and children after the parents have visited the group home becomes easier than before.

Again, all three partners were asked the same questions. All three groups answered that meaningful improvement had been achieved in all four dimensions of this criterion, but staff members believed that it had not improved as much as the parents thought it had. (See Appendix Table 2 for details).

Improvement in children's behaviour because of their involvement in this programme was recognised by all three of the partner groups, but again the parents scored the highest degree of improvement in three out of four items.

The ethnographic materials enhance the picture. A group leader said in an interview, 'There are children where the participation of their parents in the programme causes them to improve their behaviour, to work better in school and reduce violence...' One child expressed his own opinion in a letter he sent to his group care worker, 'When parents are coming to visit more often, we have high motivation to study and impress them by our achievements in school and share with them everything that is happening to us in the group home...'

Both staff members and parents identified an improvement in children's self esteem. One group leader said in an interview, 'When mothers are here, their children behave with more confidence, they are proud of their mothers, and they enjoy having a joint activity with them in the workshop...' Asked the same question, a mother said, 'My son has completely changed ... Before, when I was coming to visit him he was nervous and wouldn't listen to me ... nowadays, he is responsible, he listens to me, he feels responsible for his younger sister and he has much more confidence in himself...'

The group leaders and residential direct care workers were positive about the improvement in the children's self-esteem, although the latter scored it significantly higher than the former (See Appendix Table 3 for details).

The final question to be examined was the staff's attitudes and practices concerning parents. (See Appendix Table 4 for details).

All three groups believed that there had been a positive shift in the attitudes of staff towards the parents, but once again it was the parents who considered it more meaningful and profound than the two staff groups did.

The overall findings of this detailed evaluation research revealed that most of the project goals were attained with considerable success.

- The project succeeded in its goal of getting the parents to come to the group home regularly, and to maintain participation in the workshops geared towards improving their relationships with their children and their functioning as parents.

- The project succeeded in broadening the staff's professional activities. The group home staff moved from an approach that was only child-centred towards adding intensive work with parents.

- The project succeeded in improving the attitude of group home staff towards parents. They began to perceive parents as partners in the education of their children, even in cases where the child was placed in the home by court order.

- The project provided proof that a focused effort on improving the relationship between parents, child and group home has a significant positive impact on how the child functioned in the group home.

Thus the three project components – the weekly visits of parents and their active participation in the dynamic workshops for parents, family days in the group home and child-parent summer camps – proved capable of realising all of the project's objectives.

Discussion

The evaluation of the programme shows that the objectives were largely attained. The various activities initiated as part of the new programme had effectively reduced the feelings of dual loyalties of children in residential care. The increased presence of parents in the group home and the improvement in the staff's relationships with parents changed the children's attitudes towards the residential staff and towards being in care.

In their presentation of children in residential care, Eisikovits and Guttmann (1987) used the metaphor 'strangers on the road', to describe children's feelings while they are in residential care. We have clear evidence that for the children in the four residential group homes the conflict between their two worlds of 'home' and the 'group home' diminished markedly. This was achieved through their and their parents' own participation in the programme.

The second objective was geared to improving the relationships between parents and children, and between children and the staff of the residential group home. We found conclusive evidence of a net improvement in both.

The third objective was to try to improve parents' self-esteem and increase their competence as parents. The intensive interaction in the dynamic group sessions enabled them to raise painful issues in their lives and their feelings especially about being parents. The new experience of sharing and openly discussing with other parents their difficulties over rearing their children gave them a way to look upon themselves differently – generally to see themselves in a more positive light. The structured activities with their children, in the workshops and even more at the summer camp, brought them new intimacy with their children – a wholly new experience. Such experiences exposed them to new models they could internalise and showed them new ways of treating children. All this helped them to function better as parents.

The fourth objective dealt with changing the attitudes of the care workers and teachers to the parents. The activities empowered them and engaged them in dynamic group sessions with the parents – something they never dared to try before. Their attitude towards the parents changed completely, so that both the group leaders and residential direct care workers acknowledged the importance of parents in the children's education.

Recommendations

We can make recommendations from our findings on the following: organisation, systems, supervision, workshops, documentation and dissemination of project findings:

Organisation: the relationship between the various sub-systems within the group home needs to be strengthened so that it works as a holistic system. Since most of the programme's activities are carried out by the treatment staff (social workers), the head of this professional group is to take responsibility for coordinating all the work with the parents of children in group care.

System: although the role of the director of the group home is vital in the programmes, responsibilities should be delegated among senior staff. All staff must feel they are full participants in this kind of project in accordance with their roles. Informing the parents as soon as the child enters the group home that attendance at parent groups is an obligatory part of their basic contract will help to assure their permanent participation in the parents' workshops. A systemic perception of this pilot project is more likely to achieve the integration of activities with parents into the group home's daily schedule.

Supervision: focused training and guidance is essential for everyone operating group sessions with parents and would be of value to residential direct care workers as well.

Dynamic group workshops for parents: the various components of the programme should be carefully considered. More effort should be made to involve fathers in the parents' groups. Recognised procedures by which the principle of work with parents is implemented in all units of the group home should be established to discourage parents from dropping out of the activities.

Documentation and dissemination: each group home should establish a way to document their residential programmes. Especially effective activities and procedures that took place during the pilot project should be identified and recorded, so that the information is disseminated to staff teams through professional journals, lectures, conferences, etc. This could lead to a 'learning culture' (Shepard, 2000) among professionals in the field that will develop their practice, both as individuals and teams.

Finally, channels of communication should be strengthened with the local community welfare services from which the children are referred. This may well empower parents and children to contribute to better resolution of their problems.

References

Balster, L (1991) *Involving at-risk families in their children's education* ERIC Digest Series Number EA 58.ED326925

Beyth-Marom, R, ed (1988) *Research Methods in the Social Sciences: Regression Analysis and Analysis of Variance,* Volume 11-12 Ramat Aviv, The Open University Publications

Bulher-Niederberger, D (1999) The family ideology and its influence on residential care. In Colla, H E, ed, *Handbuch Heimerziehung und Pflegekinderwesen in Europa,* p333-341 Neuwied; Kriftel Luchterhand

Dolev, T, Aronim, H, Ben-Rabi, D, Clayman, L, Cohen, M, Traitenberg, S, and Levy, J Y (1997) *Review of Children and Youth in Israel: Policies, Programmes and Philanthropy Jerusalem,* JDC Publications

Eisikovits, R A (1980) The cultural scene of a juvenile treatment center for girls: another look *Child Care Quarterly,* 9(3):158-174

Eisikovits, Z and Guttman, E (1987) Strangers on the road: youth's experience of the community vs residential care dichotomy. In Kashti, Y and Arieli, M, eds, *Residential Settings and the Community: Congruence and Conflict,* p34-48 London, Freund, Study Group papers April 1984 Tel Aviv, Israel

Garfat, T F and McElwee, N C (2004) *Developing effective interventions with families* Cape Town, Pretext Publishing

Grupper, E (1998) Changes in the Israeli residential programs towards parents of children in care. In Yakov, M, ed, *The bridge towards recontacting staff with parents and the community,* p9-13 Tel Aviv, Administration for Rural Education and Youth Aliyah

Guttman, E (2001) *Contacts and bridges between mothers and their children: a summer camp for children in residential care together with their mothers: Evaluation report* Tel-Aviv, Yeladim, The council for children in care publications

Kahan, B (1992) The residential scene in Britain, Paper given at Tel Aviv University, School of Education

Kashty, Y, Shlaski, S, and Arieli, M (2000) The residential program and the family between rivalry and complementarity: changing concepts in the Israeli youth villages. In Kashty, Y, Shlaski, S, and Arieli, M, eds, *Youth Communities* Tel Aviv, Ramot

Laufer, Z (1991) Conserving family relationships in residential care programs for children aged 6-14 years old *Society and Welfare,* 11(2):176-183

Pasternak, R (1994) *The First Circle: residential care and the family – greenhouse or trap?* Tel Aviv, Iteav

Poso, T (1996) Family as framework: gendered residential treatment of troublesome youth *International Journal of Child and Family Welfare,* 1(1):70-82

Rot Levy, S (2003) *Report of the commission investigating basic principles concerning children and the law* Jerusalem, Ministry of Justice

Sarason, S B (1996) *Revisiting 'The Culture of The School and The Problem of Change'* London, Teachers College Press

Shepard, L A (2000) The role of assessment in the learning culture *Educational Researcher,* 29(7):414

Taylor, G R, ed (2000) *Integrating Quantitative and Qualitative Methods in Research* Oxford, University Press of America

Wiener, A (1990) *Children under human care: long term survey after children in institutions for early childhood* Jerusalem, Shoken

Appendix for chapter 9

Table 1: Research Tools and their Application Rates

Research tool	Description of activity	1st year of programme	2nd year of programme	Total
Documentation				
	Protocols of meetings	6	6	12
	Materials related to summer camps		8	8
	Feed-back sheets of parents	4	5	9
	Invitations, agenda for meetings, letters of parents and children	10	13	23
Total		20	33	55
Semi-structured interviews with:				
	National programme coordinator	2	1	3
	Directors of group homes	4	4	8
	Local coordinators	8	4	12
	Supervisors		3	3
	Group leaders	13	4	17
	Direct care workers (educational staff)		4	4
	Mothers		3	3
	Director of summer camp	1		1
Total		28	23	51
Casual interviews with:				
	Children	15	5	20
	Parents	66	10	76
	Group leaders	14	8	22
	Director of summer camp		1	1
Total		95	24	119
Observations				
	Family day in the group home	4	2	6
	Training sessions for group leaders	4	5	7
	Group session for mothers and children	11	8	19
	Group sessions for fathers and children	3		3
	Summer camp	2	2	4
	National gathering		1	1
	Steering committee meetings	6	6	12
Total		30	24	54
Questionnaires				
	Group leaders	148	112	260
	Direct group care workers	138	179	317
	Supervisors	9	14	23
Total		295	305	600
Expectation questionnaires				
	All residential staff members	69	48	117
	Group leaders		19	19
	Direct care workers (educational staff)		35	35
	Parents		27	27
Total		69	129	198

Table 2: One-way Analysis of Variance on the Items of Factor 'Attitudes towards Child-Parent Relationships'

Participants	N	Mean	SD	F	Significance
Statement:Parent increases her/his interest in what is happening with their child					
Group leaders	18	3.61	0.98		
Group care workers	22	3.68	0.84		
Parents	27	4.85	0.36		
Total	67	4.13	0.94	21.67	0.000**
Statement: Children are entitled to visit home more frequently then before					
Group leaders	17	2.76	1.25		
Group care workers	21	3.00	1.51		
Parents	25	3.96	1.10		
Total	63	3.32	1.38	5.29	0.008**
Statement: Children report better relationships with parents during visits at home					
Group leaders	17	3.41	0.80		
Group care workers	22	3.45	1.10		
Parents	26	4.69	0.84		
Total	65	3.94	1.10	14.38	0.000**
Statement: Separation of parent and child after parents' visit in the group home becomes much easier than it used to be before					
Group leaders	15	3.53	0.74		
Group care workers	21	2.57	1.17		
Parents	25	3.24	1.48		
Total	61	3.08	1.27	3.04	0.06

$P < 0.01**$

Table 3: t-test Attitudes of Workshop Group Leaders versus Residential Care Workers regarding Improvement in Children's Self-esteem

Participants	Mean Score	Standard Deviation	N	T	DF	Significance
Parents' group leaders	3.31	1.14	16			
Residential care workers	4.19	0.60	21	-303	35	0.01

$p < 0.01$

Table 4: One-way Analysis of Variance of Staff's Attitudes toward Parents

Participants	N	Mean	SD	F	Significance
Statement: There is a net improvement in staff's attitude towards parents					
Group leaders	15	3.20	1.01		
Group care workers	21	3.71	0.90		
Parents	26	4.65	0.98		
Total	62	3.98	1.12	12.12	0.000**
Statement: The group home's investment in parents has increased					
Group leaders	14	3.57	1.40		
Group care workers	21	4.14	0.79		
Parents	26	4.38	1.20		
Total	6	4.11	1.16	2.36	0.1
Statement: Professional staff are better acquainted with parents than in the past					
Group leaders	17	4.59	0.51		
Group care workers	21	4.19	0.60		
Parents	25	4.52	0.96		
Total	63	4.43	0.76	1.64	0.2
Integrative factor: residential staff's attitude towards parents					
Group leaders		3.88	0.73		
Group care workers		4.02	0.57		
Parents		4.53	0.89		
Total		4.19	0.80	4.54	0.015*

p<0.01** p<0.05 *

10

Participation of children and youth in residential child care as a matter of quality: insights into results of a practice development project

Mechthild Wolff

Context

For several years an intense debate on the implementation of the UN Convention on the Rights of the Child has taken place at international as well as European and national level. The right of participation of children and youth which is contained in Article 12[1] of the Convention is important because of its mainstreaming character. This right in the Convention has its equivalent in the reformed German national law which came into operation in 1990-91[2]. The German Federal Government has to present a report on the general development of the child and youth care system every four years.

In the year 2002 the Government stated in its 11th Child and Youth Report that the participation of children and youth is of special interest for the German child and youth care system. The report mentioned that the participation of children and youth is a component of quality development processes and participation is therefore an essential indicator of the quality of services. These observations make clear that participation is not only a question of quality but also an expression of the civil rights and the citizen status of children and young people. This overall effort to strengthen the civil rights of children and young people is the background for this chapter, which deals with the issue of the participation of children and youth in residential child care in Germany.

Project approach: the right of a self-determined user perspective of quality

The chapter reflects the experience and knowledge gained through the project Participation as a Quality Standard for Residential Child and Youth Care. The project was carried out in 2005 over one year. It was initiated by SOS-Kinderdorf e.V. Germany and the Internationale Gesellschaft für erzieherische Hilfen e.V. (IGfH), the German branch of the International Fédération of Communautés Educatives (FICE) and managed by the Social Work Faculty at the Landshut University of Applied Sciences. The goal of the project was to define the quality of participation in residential child care from a user perspective, and to conjointly compile with young people what they think constitutes successful participation in the practice of residential child care. We wanted to understand what they consider as indicators for successful participation in their everyday life.

When exploring what the word 'participation' meant, we were impressed by how many definitions we found in the literature and how many models of participation were described by this word. The scale of Hart and Gernert (1995, p16) is useful. They defined models of participation on a scale between heteronomy and autonomy, with self-government the most autonomous form to realise one's own wishes, ideas and interests. Their detailed differentiation shows that at all levels of the scale the role and intensity of autonomy between children and adults differ.

Selbstverwaltung = self-government
Selbstbestimmung = self-determination
Mitbestimmung = codetermination
Mitwirkung = contribution
Zugewiesen, informiert = assigned, informed
Teilhabe = taking part
Alibi-Teilhabe = quasi-participation
Dekoration = decoration
Fremdbestimmung = heteronomy (Hart and Gernert, 1995, p16)

Other attempts to define models of participation concluded that the scale can range from an absence of participation through quasi-participation to the presence of participation. In every case participation is considered an empowerment and activating process (see Petersen, 2002).

We wanted to find out more about the self-determined definition of successful participation from the viewpoint of young people, taking account of these stages of participation.

Our methods

First, a literature search within the scope of the project was carried out, in which the various participation discussions in the German education and training system were examined in respect to their problem zones (http://people.fh-landshut.de/~hartig/ergebnisse/index.html). We also looked for institutions which established models of participation in everyday life and collected them as good practice examples. We included them in our recommendations here.

To learn more about the subjective perspective of young people, we conducted a weekend workshop with fifteen young people and their carers from six German residential child and youth care facilities that we had researched and identified as operating good models of participation. We held brainstorming sessions with the young people, with subsequent cluster creation and ranking phases, as well as group discussions. The young people themselves produced a video on the theme of participation and other creative visualisations resulting from their discussion. We considered such creative and experimental forms of working with young people as a way to give them the opportunity to express their ideas. What came out of this experimental approach gave us the basis for our recommendations for implementing participation, documented below. The analysis of the results is the basis for a new project: a representative survey in residential child and youth care institutions throughout Germany. This chapter documents only some of our findings. (For further information see: http://people.fh-landshut.de/~hartig/ergebnisse/index.html)

Results of the literature analysis

At a federal as well as local level, participation by young people is of great interest in politics and all educational institutions such as school and day care (Bartscher, 1998; Bruner *et al*, 1999; Knauer *et al*, 2003). We found many national organisations which promote information platforms in the internet about the rights of children and young people and especially their right to participation. They carry information about opportunities for young people to get involved in political affairs and to participate in a democratic culture. Chat rooms for young people are being promoted and organisations invest much money supporting projects and local activities.

We also found project reports which deal with the participation of young people in national and local politics. Some of the initiatives at national level are for example: *Bertelsmann Stiftung, Deutsches Kinderhilfswerk, Bundeszentrale für politische Bildung, Aktion Jugendschutz*. Some can be found in the internet at: www.projekt-p.de; www.dkhw.de; www.kinderpolitik.de, www.mitwirkung.net. After analysing a good many concepts we found that the underlying philosophy is that the idea of participation be accepted as a model idea for democracy and civil society. Participation is identified as a normative principle for the realisation of democracy. It therefore receives acceptance and attention and is combined with high expectations at all levels of society.

Participation in residential care needs substantial development in implementation in everyday life

We found that participation in residential child care has a long tradition in Germany. There is historical evidence of models of participation in 'children's republics' all over Europe (see Kamp, 1995). We also found that participation was an issue in the events around the general reform processes of the child and youth care system at the end of the 1970s and 1980s in Germany. Major changes in the child care system had been initiated by student revolts in residential youth homes. Students criticised bad conditions, lack of education for carers and lack of democratic culture in overly large residential institutions (Arbeitsgruppe Heimreform, 2000).

At the end of the 1990s the administrative system demanded that participation in residential care (*Bundersarbeitgemeinscheft der Landesjugendämter*, 1998) be implemented. Along with political pressure, intense debate ensued about participation as a concept for democracy and as a general basis for residential child care, with some good practice examples of participation models in action (Kriener and Petersen, 1999; Kriener, 1999). By the end of the 1990s authors were urging that participation be seen as a matter of quality in the caring process (see Blandow, 1999; Blandow *et al*, 1999). Much energy and money was invested in processes of quality management in institutions, so it is surprising how little attention the implementation of participation models has received up to the present time.

It is, moreover, surprising that there are so few studies about the dissemination of participation in the child and youth care system in Germany. We found only three empirical studies which deal with the subject of participation models in child care institutions (Pluto and Mamier *et al*, 2003; Babic and Lengenmayer, 2004; Gragert *et al*, 2005). An initiative established by the German Government which tries to improve the procedure of decision making in the administrative planning process (*Hilfeplanung*) (www.dji.de) is now under way. Our project focuses not on the decision making procedure but on the everyday caring process in pedagogical settings.

All three of the empirical studies prove that carers identify the idea of parti-cipation as an essential concept and an important value in educational settings. However, a closer look at implementation in every day life reveals that participation remains dependent on the goodwill of the carers. It seems that there is a big gap between the perspectives of professionals and the definitions and views of young people. Professionals identify a need for parti-cipation but children and young people appear to have different perceptions of the implementation of participation.

Results of our workshop with young people from residential homes

At the workshop with fifteen young people aged 15 to 18 years from six child and youth care institutions in Germany we explored what young people asso-ciate with participation in their youth care institutions. In order to collect their ideas and views they set up a brainstorming session, and used clustering to collect their peers' ideas, which they arranged in order of importance. In answer to the question, 'What do you consider indicators for successful parti-cipation in your residential youth care institution?' they ranked the factors as following.

Indicators for successful participator as ranked by 15 young people

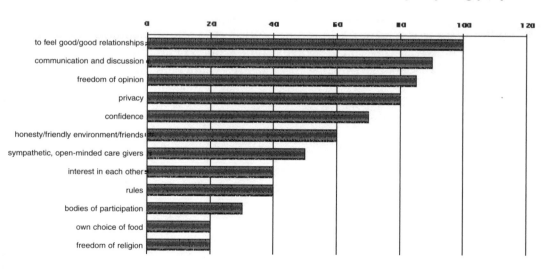

It was clear that the young people's ideas were strongly drawn from, and affected by, their everyday experiences. They based their arguments on their experience with carers and their peer group in their residential settings. They stated that the relationship with their carers was the most important in-dicator for successful participation. They wanted to feel participation as an honest and authentic attitude of the carers who should be good friends and who should accept them. Communication and discussions and the oppor-tunity to express their own opinions were also high in their ranking list. Values of privacy, confidence, security, trust, comfort, well-being and integration seemed far more important to them than formalised models of participation.

It was interesting that the young people associated specific personal charac-teristics with participative carers. They defined carers who have a participa-tive attitude as being honest, friendly and open-minded. The first indicators in the ranking list proved that young people associated 'soft indicators' with participation, and they made strong connections between participative approaches and the personal demeanour and emotional behaviour of carers.

We can conclude that young people want to experience the implementation of participation in everyday life situations, such as in the question of decorating their rooms and making decisions about groceries and meals. So the strongest indicator for successful participation seems to be the feeling that participation is an authentic attitude of professionals who express it in an honest manner in their relationships with young people in residential child care.

Results of the workshop: participation requires a specific climate

The views expressed by the young people can be grouped into three major indicators for successful participation in residential youth care from a user perspective:

- **Atmosphere**: as one young person said, 'You have to feel well in your home'.
- **Social relations**: as one young person said, 'A good relationship with my care giver is important for me to feel safe'.
- **General condition**: as one young person said, '... everything which supports participation is important and complements one another'.

Looking at all the different levels of indicators and especially at this last state-ment, we can see that the implementation of participation needs a general and holistic approach which covers all of these aspects. We had already found references for this idea in the literature research: a practice development project which was operated by a big German child and youth care institution in the north of the country implemented a model of participation in a long-term organisational development process (*Diakonieverbund Schweichen e.v.,*

2006). In systematic proceedings in the institution all care givers – other employees as well as carers – were being involved in the development of children's rights protocols and the establishment of grievance procedures for children and young people.

That project proved that the implementation process requires the involvement of all people and the right for all people to participate – no matter what their status or function in the institution. The people in charge of the project argued that there is a strong need for developing a specific 'culture of participation' in organisations. In our own project in Landshut we also found from our discussions with young people and professionals that personal and professional attitudes cannot be changed by issuing strict orders or imposing implementation plans for participation models. The process of implementation needs to incorporate a concept of participation, to give everybody the chance to identify with new values and attitudes concerning participation and to implement them in their communication and interaction with children and young people.

In publications and project examples we found that the indicators for successful participation were:

- Implementation needs a culture of participation.

- Implementation needs a professional and personally positive attitude towards participation.

Since we found many 'soft indicators' which were connected to emotional aspects in the settings and relationships between professionals and young people, we added a third indicator to our list: implementation is also a question of creating a social climate which allows the chance to experience participation in all interactions and proceedings in everyday life. Consequently we concluded:

- Implementation needs a climate of participation.

We integrated all indicators for successful participation in the idea of a 'conditioner for participation'. The conditioner needs all the mentioned requirements in order to produce a climate of participation. In our analysis we consider a professional attitude and a culture of participation as the basis for a specific climate.

The 'Participation Conditioner'

We learned from our findings that, from a user perspective, the quality of participation is dependent on the social climate predominating in an institution. The specific social climate based on participation can only emerge if all indicators of the 'conditioner for participation' are regarded as equal and necessary organizational processes.

Recommendations and good practice examples as quality indicators for participation

From the basis of our workshop results with the young people, our workshop with carers and directors from the six facilities, our literature research, and our examination of participation models and projects in Germany we developed recommendations for participation. (For further recommendations see http://people.fh-landshut.de/~hartig/ergebnisse/index.html):

■ **Professionals leave the defining of participation to the children and young people and recognise them as recipients, users and also experts in relation to services.**

As the perspectives and expectations of children and youth and professionals are not always identical, professionals must, above all, recognise how children and youth define participation and their wishes regarding participation. As children and youth are the best experts on their residential care experience, they can also best judge the quality of services.

This can be put into effect through good practice examples such as programmed workshops with children and youth, and regular surveys and inquiries of the children and youth, amongst others.

■ **Professionals possess aptitude for participation.**

Participation can be a matter of degree. If the forms of the heteronomy increase to self-determination levels, professionals must have basic knowledge of democratic values, as well as personal aptitude, to convey cooperation and ultimately to substantiate these values in daily functions. Children and youth require adults who are personally concerned to help them and who come across as authentic, empathetic and friendly partners.

This can be put into effect through good practice examples such as:

- – creating training standards for employees to translate participation into everyday life,
- – participation being a theme in regular training and workshops,
- – providing resources for reflection on professional point of views and personal attitudes towards participation.

■ **Professionals reflect the general educational principle of participation in their daily activities.**

For the active, practical participation of children, youth and professionals in the daily life of residential child and youth care facilities, professionals must be agreed on the necessity of participation as a general pedagogical principle.

This can be put into effect through good practice examples such as:

- agreeing that participation is a criterion for the quality of service
- adopting educational competences which collectively support participation in practice
- examining all educational interactions and interventions in the light of participation.

■ **Professionals inform children and youth about all relevant concerns and rights.**

Young people need to be informed about their own rights and participation. Therefore they should be comprehensively informed through age-appropriate residential care and education, that is, in accordance with their development. The right to information also entails the free access to the internet.

This can be put into effect through good practice examples such as providing:

- leaflets with standards for children and youth, information brochures and discussions
- internet access for children and youth
- information events for children and youth
- information on bulletin boards.

■ **Facilities in residential child care develop a participation culture.**

As implementing participation in daily life can only be motivated and ensured through long-term processes, the development of a participation culture is necessary. A participation culture can be stimulated through concrete participation-producing measures, and employees, as well as the children and young people, must be open to translating opportunities into experiential participation.

This can be out into effect through good practice examples such as:

- drawing up ways of participating in quality manuals
- operationalising of participation in educational concepts
- developing practice outlines concerning participation.

■ **Facilities in residential child care develop a participation climate.**

As participation is expressed in the quality of human relations and in social conditions, facilities have to take a long-term approach in creating a participation climate, and be prepared to accept criticism and to change.

This can be realised through good practice examples such as:

– conferences for children, youth and their carers
– collective work on processes and participation projects
– training in giving positive feed-back and forms of review
– collective training under democratic rules
– measures of quality development and human resources development.

■ **Facilities in residential child care develop a participation model.**

As participation requires a long-term and continuous negotiation process for all those involved, measures for organisational and personnel development should be promoted.

This can be put into effect through good practice examples such as:

– participation models
– children's rights protocols.

■ **Facilities in residential child care implement their general model of participation in a binding system requiring commitment to participation.**

Because the guarantee of participation relies on a secure framework, binding arrangements and participation possibilities should be institutionally negotiated and implemented. This concept should be oriented to the UN Convention on the Rights of the Child and the human and social rights which apply.

This can be implemented through good practice examples such as:

– binding organisational ordinances and statutes for participation bodies
– a requirement to apply participation in accordance with German law (§ 36 KJHG).

Special thanks to project staff member Sabine Hartig for her contribution to this article.

Note

1 Article 12 of the UN Convention on the Rights of the Child includes:

1. States parties shall assure to the child who is capable of forming his or her own views the right to express those views freely in all matters affecting the child, the views of the child being given due weight in accordance with the age and maturity of the child.

2. For this purpose, the child shall in particular be provided the opportunity to be heard in any judicial and administrative proceedings affecting the child, either directly, or through a representative or an appropriate body, in a manner consistent with the procedural rules of national law.

2 Paragraph § 8 (1) in the German Child and Youth Services Act (Kinder- und Jugendhilfgesetz KJHG/SGB VIII) states, 'In accordance with personal maturity and development children and young persons are to be involved in all decisions of statutory youth services concerning them'. In German law this § is considered to be the paragraph with most impact. Moreover there are additional paragraphs (§ 36 SGB VIII, § 5, § 9 e.g.) which make clear that children and youth have the right to participate in all proceedings.

References

Arbeitsgruppe Heimreform (2000) *Aus der Geschichte lernen: Analyse der Heimreform in Hessen* (1968-1983) Frankfurt/Main, Internationale Gesellschaft für erzieherische Hilfen,

Babic, B and Lengenmayer, K, eds (2004) *Partizipation in der Heimerziehung Abschlussbericht der explorativen Studie zu den formalen Strukturen der Beteiligung von Kindern und Jugendlichen in ausgewählten Einrichtungen der stationären Erziehungshilfe in Bayern* München, Bayerisches Landesjugendamt

Bartscher, M (1998) *Partizipation von Kindern in der Kommunalpolitik* Freiburg im Breisgau, Lambertus

Blandow, J (1999) Beteiligung als Qualitätsmerkmal in der Heimerziehung. In Kriener, M and Petersen, K, eds, *Beteiligung in der Jugendhilfepraxis: sozialpädagogische Strategien zur Partizipation in Erziehungshilfen und bei Vormundschaften*, p45-62 Münster, Votum

Blandow, J, Gintzel, U and Hansbauer, P (1999) *Partizipation als Qualitätsmerkmal in der Heimerziehung: Eine Diskussionsgrundlage* Münster, Votum

Bruner, C F, Winklhofer, U and Zinser, C (1999) *Beteiligung von Kindern und Jugendlichen in der Kommune – Ergebnisse einer bundesweiten Erhebung* München, Bundesministerium für Familie, Senioren, Frauen und Jugend/Deutsches Jugendinstitut e.V.

Bundesarbeitsgemeinschaft der Landesjugendämter (1998) Positionspapier 'Beteiligung von Kindern und Jugendlichen' Aalen, Kreisjugendring Ostalb

Diakonieverbund Schweicheln e.V., ed (2006) *Erziehung braucht eine Kultur der Partizipation Umsetzung und Ergebnisse eines Modellprojekts in der Erziehungshilfe* Hiddenhausen, Diakonieverbund Schweicheln e. V.

Gragert, N, Pluto, L, Santen, E van and Seckinger, M (2005) *Entwicklungen (teil)stationärer Hilfen zur Erziehung – Ergebnisse und Analysen der Einrichtungsbefragung 2004* München, Deutsches Jugendinstitut e. V.

Hart, R and Gernert, W (1995) Stufenleiter als ein Kriterium für die Einschätzung von Partizipationsmodellen In Schröer, R, ed, *Kinder reden mit! Beteiligung an Politik, Stadtplanung und Stadtgestaltung* Weinheim; Basel, Beltz

Kamp, J-M (1995) *Kinderrepubliken Geschichte, Praxis und Theorie radikaler Selbstregierung in Kinder- und Jugendheimen* Leske und Budrich, Opladen

Knauer, R, Friedrich, B, Herrmann, T and Liebler, B (2004) *Partizipationsprojekte mit Kindern und Jugendlichen in der Kommune Vom Beteiligungsprojekt zum demokratischen Gemeinwesen* Wiesbaden, VS Verlag für Sozialwissenschaften

Kriener, M (1999) Beteiligung als Chance für mehr Demokratie in der Heimerziehung In Kriener, M and Petersen, K, eds, *Beteiligung in der Jugendhilfepraxis: sozialpädagogische Strategien zur Partizipation in Erziehungshilfen und bei Vormundschaften*, p112-129 Münster, Votum

Kriener, M and Petersen, K, eds (1999) *Beteiligung in der Jugendhilfepraxis: sozialpädagogische Strategien zur Partizipation in Erziehungshilfen und bei Vormundschaften Münster*, Votum

Petersen, K (2002) Partizipation. In Schröer, W, Struck, N and Wolff, M, eds, *Handbuch Kinder- und Jugendhilfe*, p909-924 Weinheim; München, Juventa-Verlag

Pluto, L, Mamier, J, Santen, E van, Seckinger, M and Zink, G (2003) *Partizipation im Kontext erzieherischer Hilfen – Anspruch und Wirklichkeit Eine empirische Studie* München, Das Deutsche Jugendinstitut e. V.

11

The care system for homeless youth in the Netherlands: perceptions of youngsters through a peer-research approach[1]

Marc J. Noom and Micha de Winter

Introduction

Homeless youth in the western world are estimated to be in this situation for three to five years on average (Ploeg and Scholte, 1997; Korf *et al*, 1999). Often these youngsters have a long history of youth care before and during their homelessness. This prolonged process of care is detrimental to the physical and mental health of these youngsters. The primary aim of the present study is to reveal how homeless youth evaluate the care system. We wanted to include homeless youngsters in this research as participants through a peer-research approach.

Homeless youth in western countries can be defined as young people aged 12 to 25, who have no regular place to stay, living sometimes on the streets, sometimes in the houses of friends or family, and sometimes in accommodation for homeless youth (Noom and Winter, 2001; Ploeg and Scholte, 1997). According to Ploeg and Scholte homelessness often starts with running away or being sent away from home (whether leaving parents or partner), from a foster family, or from a residential centre. Most of these youngsters return to their homes, but a small proportion does not and they stay with friends, as squatters, or out on the streets. Sometimes they stay at a youth hostel, a shelter, or at a trained housing centre. This cyclic process is typical for homeless youth.

Factors related to youth homelessness can be categorised as individual, social or societal. At the individual level, a lack of autonomy plays a key role in the emergence of homelessness. A central developmental task for adolescents is to develop the ability to give direction to their own life (Noom, 1999), by learning how to make decisions (cognitive autonomy), developing self-confidence (emotional autonomy), and learning how to develop a strategy to reach a specific goal (behavioural autonomy). Several studies have shown that homeless youngsters experience difficulties in their cognitive functioning and sense of mastery (eg a high external locus of control: Ploeg et al, 1991), their emotional stability (eg a low self-esteem: Kurtz et al, 1991), and their strategic behaviour in dealing with problematic situations (eg ineffective coping and lack of ego-control: Ploeg et al, 1991). In sum, inadequate adolescent autonomy increases the risk of being unable to deal with problems and to become homeless.

At the social level, attachment is a determinant of youth homelessness. An important developmental task during adolescence is to achieve and maintain attachment relationships with adults (in particular parents) and peers (Allen and Land, 1999). Many homeless youngsters come from severely disturbed multi-problem families with high levels of neglect and family crisis, where parents practise devastating methods in their upbringing of their children (Kurtz et al, 1991; Ploeg and Scholte, 1997). A history of child maltreatment and abuse is common (Powers et al, 2003). Such family circumstances limit the development of the youngsters' ability to connect to others to build a significant relationship. Being unable to connect to others increases the risk of becoming homeless.

Social-economical factors also have an impact on homelessness. Poverty, lack of affordable houses, limited educational prospects, and unemployment all add to the likelihood of becoming homeless (Ploeg and Scholte, 1997). The present study deals primarily with the individual and social factors.

The care-system for homeless youth in western European countries varies from low-intensive approaches to very intensive approaches. First, there are outreach programmes (street corner work), where the primary aim is to establish some kind of contact. Once initial contact is established, the youngsters are encouraged to accept more extensive types of help. Secondly, there are emergency shelters. In day-care centres and sleep centres youngsters can stay during the day or night, and can shower, wash their clothes, and have a meal. A third type of help is non-residential or outpatient care offering practical, physical, and mental help. Finally, there is residential care, where extensive counselling is provided in pensions and trained housing centres.

In spite of the comprehensive care system, homeless youth encounter numerous difficulties in finding their way back into society. It can take several years before these youngsters can make a successful transition into young adulthood and live on their own again (Korf *et al*, 2000). From a pedagogical perspective, one of the reasons for this inefficiency can be found in the relationship between adolescents and adults: the tension between autonomy and attachment (Noom, 1999; Noom *et al*, 2001). Adolescents are focused on developing abilities that enable them to function as autonomous individuals. At the same time they are developing attachments to significant others. Adults (parents, educators, youth workers) have to respond to these needs adequately. The striving of the young person for autonomy has to be supported by a structural approach based on encouragement and stimulation of free exploration. The striving for attachment has to be responded to with warmth and acceptance.

Peer-research is a specific form of collaborative research in which the research subjects are at the same time research participants (Cashmore, 2002). In the specific kind of participatory action research used here, the participants are involved in both the research and the implementation of the findings. Involvement in such research can entail specifying the research question, developing an instrument for data-collection, or interpreting the results. Implementation can involve developing practical implications or new policies. This chapter describes our experiences with homeless youngsters as participating peer-researchers.

Procedure

A group of twenty-two Dutch homeless youngsters (eighteen boys and four girls, aged 15 to 24) was recruited through several organisations of professional care in three cities in the Netherlands: Amsterdam, Rotterdam and The Hague. In the first two sessions they were informed about the aim of the project and what it was that they were expected to do. They were invited to participate in research on the opinions of homeless youth about the care-system. An interview script was developed and discussed with the youngsters. During a weekend the youngsters were trained to conduct this interview. The youngsters were then asked to collect ten interviews in the city where they lived and to return these at specified times, when a collaborator of the research would be available to receive them.

The interview

A semi-structured interview was developed together with these homeless youngsters around ten domains: housing, physical health, mental health, contact with relatives, contact with friends, education, work, income, encounters with the police and the justice system, and leisure activities. The purpose of the interview was to make an inventory in each domain of (a) the present situation, (b) whether they think that social workers should help them in that domain, (c) whether social workers actually do help them, (d) which aspects of this care are efficient, and (e) which aspects of this care are inefficient. These questions were asked orally, and the answers were written down by the interviewer. The interviewers were paid $5 for each completed interview.

Subjects

In total 189 homeless youngsters were interviewed, 142 (75%) boys and 47 (25%) girls aged between 14 and 24. The average age was 19.6 years (SD = 1,82). The background of forty-two percent of the youngsters (76) was Dutch, 16 per cent (30) Surinamese or from the Dutch Antilles, 9 per cent (18) Moroccan, 4 per cent (8) Turkish, and 29 per cent (54) other non-western backgrounds. Both the proportion of boys to girls and the proportion of different ethnic groups corresponds with recent representative research on homeless adolescents in the Netherlands (Korf *et al*, 2000). Half the youngsters interviewed (49%) had been homeless for up to one and a half years, another 46 per cent of the youngsters had been homeless for up to five years, and 5 per cent had been homeless for over five years.

Results (see Appendix for detailed results)

The interview started with a list of the ten domains. The homeless youngsters were asked if they thought that social workers should help them with problems in these domains (see Table 1 and Table 2). Chi-square tests were performed to test significant differences between boys and girls, and between adolescents with a Dutch origin and those with other ethnic backgrounds.

When it comes to basic needs (housing, education, work, income, police and judiciary), the vast majority of the adolescents (74% to 95%) argued that social workers should be available for help of this kind. Chi-square tests revealed no significant differences on lines of gender or ethnicity. The help actually received in the domain of basic needs is a bit lower, ranging from 42 per cent to 79 per cent. Girls report significantly less help in education and work (33% and 34% respectively) than boys (52% and 55% respectively).

For physical and mental health needs roughly two thirds (59% to 65%) had to receive help from social workers. In the domain of physical health a significantly higher percentage of boys (70%) than girls (51%) argued that they should be helped. The actual help given in this domain ranged from 47 per cent to 53 per cent, with a significant gender difference: boys reported that they received help more often (52%) than the girls reported (30%).

The results for social needs – contact with family and friends, leisure activities – revealed a different picture. Roughly one third (28% to 47%) had the opinion that social workers should be available for help in this domain. The actual help that the youngsters said they received ranged from 13 per cent to 32 per cent. For both desired help and actual help no significant differences were found in terms of gender or ethnicity.

Basic needs

With respect to housing most of the homeless youngsters (79%) were positive about the efforts of their social workers, reporting that the social workers found them a permanent place to live (39%) or a temporary place to stay (30%) (see Table 3). A minority of 21 per cent indicated that they received no help from social workers (14%) or that they had to do everything themselves (3%). The most important improvements needed were more houses (26%), quicker help (25%) and a bigger effort from the social worker (11%). Furthermore, a total of 17 per cent said that they did not know any possible improvements.

In education 47 per cent reported positive views about the work of the social workers in looking for a school (26%) and stimulating youngsters to stay there (12%), but 53 per cent of the youngsters stated that the professionals had not helped them. For some no education was being undertaken (27%); others believed that it was not the task of social workers to help in this domain (12%). More support when seeking education (11%) and more individual attention when in school (9%) were identified as possible improvements. Almost half (48%) said that they did not see any ways of improving the care they received.

In the domain of work the statistics are similar: 49 per cent were positive about the work of the professionals, 22 per cent said they helped them to find a job, and 12 per cent that they had helped by providing stimulation and motivation, but 51 per cent of the youngsters received no help with work. One reason given was that it was not the responsibility of the professionals to help them in this domain (20%). Possible improvements identified here were more support (9%), more jobs (5%) and better advice (5%). A group of 41 per cent offered no suggestions for improvement.

In the domain of income, 75 per cent of the youngsters claimed that they were being helped. Social workers were helping them to make financial plans (37%), arrange benefits (20%), and solve financial debts (12%), but 25 per cent of the youngsters received no help: they arranged their own income (7%) and social workers did not help them (7%). Improvements suggested were a bigger budget (16%), quicker help (12%), and more cooperation between the homeless youngster and the professional (8%). For 32 per cent no improvements were required.

Finally, when it came to help in the domain of police and judicial affairs only 42 per cent reported that they were helped. Social workers tried to mediate when there were some problems for 15 per cent of the youngsters, and tried actively to solve the problems for 11 per cent, but the professionals did not help 58 per cent of the youngsters in this area, either because there were no problems (34%) or because they did not see it as the responsibility of their social worker to help them (12%). The improvements identified were to give these problems a higher priority (7%) and to provide more support (3%). A large group (57%) of the youngsters did not see any potential for improvements.

Health needs
In the domain of physical and mental health, the basic function of social workers was to refer the adolescents to professional doctors. Forty-six per cent reported being positive about the work of the social workers caring for their physical health. They looked for a doctor (18%) or helped them to go to a doctor (12 per cent). In some cases (11%) the agency had their own doctor.

About 54 per cent of the youngsters stated that the professionals gave no help. Some said this was because they helped themselves (33%). Others maintained that they had no problems (9%) or that it was not the task of social workers to help with their physical health (9%). They identified as potential improvements that health care should be better organised (11%) and wanted more attention to be paid to physical problems (4%). Yet no fewer than 58 per cent said that they did not see any ways to improve physical health care.

In the mental domain there was both appreciation and a request for simple straightforward care, such as talking about problems, providing support, and giving advice. On the other hand, there was some reluctance among the adolescents to seek or accept help, because they did not want others dealing with their own problems. About 53 per cent of the youngsters claimed to be positive about the efforts of social workers, who generally talked with them

(21%), referred youngsters to other sources of help (17%) and, more specifically, listened and gave support and advice (12%).

About 47 per cent of the youngsters were negative about the care they received. They argued that social workers were unavailable to talk with (16%), or did not ask about their problems (10%). An improvement suggested by 34 per cent of the youngsters was that they should receive more attention for their problems, whereas 6 per cent wanted time to cool down, and no improvements were identified by 36 per cent.

Social needs
When they spoke about contact with family and friends, and about leisure activities, the general feeling among the adolescents was that this was their own concern. It was their view that most of the time social workers should not and could not interfere. The youngsters argued that they wanted to decide for themselves whether or not to see their parents, and who to choose as their friends. However, there was also a substantial group that appreciated help with re-establishing contact with parents, and a smaller group that appreciated help with making contact with peers.

Conclusion
What we see is a mismatch between the demands of the youngsters on the one hand and the demands of the social workers on the other hand. The professional care system for homeless youth has traditionally emphasised the importance of the ideas of the professional worker while overlooking the responsibility of the client. The clients feel dependent on the social workers and tend to adopt their proposals, while forgetting their own responsibility. Together, these tendencies enhance a hierarchical relationship which has an unbalanced division of responsibilities.

In the discussions between homeless youngsters, social workers and policy makers better correspondence was called for between the demands of the youngsters and the demands of the social workers. A prerequisite for this correspondence is open communication about the problems, which allows both youngsters and workers to speak frankly about the issues. A second condition the young people identified is the necessity to be able to discuss possible solutions. The youngsters and the social workers each have their own ideas about the kind of help needed. It should not be up to the social worker to be responsible for the choice of a specific plan of action, but it should not be solely up to the youngsters either themselves to decide what help they need. Both have their own responsibilities: the social workers have a good overview of possible plans of action, the youngsters have an opinion about what they think is necessary for them to be able to live their lives as independent individuals. In a discussion which takes account of both viewpoints, agreement could be reached on an individually tailored care programme. If no agreement can be reached, a procedure needs to be developed to find a way out that is acceptable for both parties.

Homeless youth encounter numerous difficulties in finding their way back into society. It can take several years before they make a successful developmental transition into young adulthood and live on their own again (Korf *et al*, 2000). The reasons for their inability lie in both the individual and the social domain. Homeless youth often do not experience feelings of trust towards professional workers or adults in general (Korf *et al*, 1999). Their negative experiences with parents, teachers, and social workers have made them deeply suspicious of any form of help or guidance. Social workers for their part experience difficulties in finding a way of stimulating youngsters' autonomy and creating an atmosphere of acceptance. If they cannot provide a safe environment, they may delay the healthy transition into adulthood.

A parallel can be drawn between the parent-adolescent relationship and the relationship between social worker and homeless adolescent. Both parent and social worker attempt to change and direct the behaviour of the adolescent. Their efforts are characterised by a structural dimension and a support dimension (Maccoby and Martin, 1983).

The structural dimension has two poles: encouragement of autonomy versus firm control. Encouragement of autonomy means an attitude of stimulating independent exploration. Firm control describes an approach of strict rules and harsh discipline.

The support dimension also has two poles: acceptance versus rejection. Acceptance involves handling children and adolescents in a loving and child-centred way, and so creating a strong emotional bond. Rejection is characterised by adults being emotionally neglectful or dismissive. Both parents and social workers try to find the optimal combination of structure and support so they can direct the adolescents' behaviour in a context of safety and emotional support. The results of the present study seem to indicate that social workers are primarily focused on providing structure for homeless adolescents, whereas it is equally important to pay attention to providing a safe environment.

Another parallel of the parent-adolescent relationship to the relationship between social worker and homeless adolescent is the process of renegotiation of roles (Youniss and Smollar, 1995). For adolescents to be able to develop into independent individuals a change is required from a hierarchical to an egalitarian relationship: adolescents feel an increasing need to make their own decisions.

However, many institutions for homeless youth still work with a strictly organised system based on their own convenience. Dialogue is needed, which places equal emphasis on the demands of the youngsters and those of the social workers. Greater autonomy can be achieved by doing more to enhance autonomy and attachment. This can be achieved by making homeless young people aware of their own responsibilities and discussing all the relevant issues with them – both the inventory of problems and the proposed solutions. Greater attachment can be achieved by providing safety and thereby enhancing youngsters' capacity to connect to others. Adolescents will always live in a social world where they will have to be able to relate to other people, and this needs to be dealt with more effectively in the professional care system, especially since homeless adolescents have so often had a bad start in developing a meaningful relationship with significant others, such as parents, teachers and social workers.

Note
1 This study was supported by Zorgonderzoek Nederland (ZON), a Dutch national institute for research in physical and mental health.

References

Allen, J and Land, D (1999) Attachment in adolescence. In Cassidy, J and Shaver, P R, eds, *Handbook of attachment: Theory, research, and clinical applications*, p319-335 London, Guilford Press

Cashmore, J (2002) Promoting the participation of children and young people in care *Child Abuse and Neglect*, 26:837-847

Korf, J, Diemel, S, Ripper, H and Nabben, T (2000) *Het Volgende Station Zwerfjongeren in Nederland 1999* Amsterdam, Thela Thesis

Kurtz, P D, Jarvis, S V and Kurtz, G (1991) The problems of homeless youth: empirical findings and human service issues *Social Work*, 36:309-314

Maccoby, E E and Martin, J A (1983) Socialization in the context of the family: parent-child interaction In Hetherington, E M, ed, *Handbook of Child Psychology: Socialization, Personality and Social Development*, Volume 4, p1-102 New York, Wiley, Fourth edition

Mounier, C and Andujo, E (2003) Defensive functioning of homeless youth in relation to experiences of child maltreatment and cumulative victimization *Child Abuse and Neglect*, 27:1187-1204

Noom, M (1999) *Adolescent autonomy: Characteristics and correlates* Delft, Eburon

Noom, M and Winter, M de (2001) *Op zoek naar verbondenheid Zwerfjongeren aan het woord over de verbetering van de hulpverlening* Utrecht, Universiteit Utrecht and het Nederlands Platform Zwerfjongeren

Noom, M J, Dekovic, M and Meeus, W (2001) Conceptual analysis and measurement of adolescent autonomy *Journal of Youth and Adolescence*, 30:577-595

Ploeg, J D van der, Gaemers, J and Hoogendam, P H (1991) *Zwervende jongeren* Leiden, DSWO Press

Ploeg, J D van der and Scholte, E M (1997) *Homeless Youth* London, Sage

Powers, J L, Eckenrode, J and Jaklitsch, B (1990) Maltreatment among runaway and homeless youth *Child Abuse and Neglect*, 14:87-98

Youniss, J and Smollar, J (1985) *Adolescent relations with mothers, fathers and friends Chicago*, Chicago University Press

Appendix for chapter 11

Table 1: Opinions of homeless young people about the help wanted from social workers

Should social workers help you in this domain?

Domain	Total N = 189 (%) yes	Males N = 142 (%) yes	Females N = 47 (%) yes	Dutch N = 76 (%) yes	Ethnic N = 108 (%) yes	Comparison of M/F X2 (p value)		Comparison of D/E X2 (p value)	
Basic Needs:									
Finding a house	179 (95%)	134 (95%)	45 (96%)	73 (96%)	101 (94%)	0.13	-0.71	0.56	-0.46
Education	153 (81%)	115 (81%)	38 (81%)	65 (86%)	84 (78%)	0.00	-0.98	1.74	-0.19
Work	166 (88%)	126 (89%)	40 (85%)	68 (91%)	94 (87%)	0.62	-0.43	0.57	-0.45
Income	171 (91%)	128 (90%)	43 (92%)	69 (91%)	97 (90%)	0.08	-0.79	0.05	-0.83
Police/Judiciary	138 (74%)	104 (74%)	34 (72%)	51 (68%)	83 (78%)	0.07	-0.79	2.08	-0.15
Health Needs:									
Physical Health	123 (65%)	99 (70%)	24 (51%)	49 (65%)	70 (65%)	5.40	-0.02	0.00	-0.96
Mental Health	110 (59%)	85 (61%)	25 (54%)	48 (63%)	60 (57%)	0.82	-0.37	0.79	-0.38
Social Needs:									
Contact Family	89 (47%)	72 (51%)	17 (36%)	37 (49%)	52 (48%)	2.99	-0.08	0.00	-0.94
Contact Friends	52 (28%)	42 (30%)	10 (22%)	22 (29%)	30 (28%)	1.07	-0.30	0.02	-0.89
Leisure Activities	52 (28%)	43 (30%)	9 (19%)	24 (32%)	26 (24%)	2.19	-0.14	1.27	-0.26

Table 2: Opinions of homeless young people about the actual help of social workers

Do social workers help you in this domain?

Domain	Total N = 189 (%) yes	Males N = 142 (%) yes	Females N = 47 (%) yes	Dutch N = 76 (%) yes	Ethnic N = 108 (%) yes	Comparison of M/F X2 (p value 2-s)		Comparison of D/E X2 (p value 2-s)	
Basic Needs:									
Finding a house	148 (79%)	112 (80%)	36 (77%)	58 (78%)	88 (82%)	0.25	-0.62	0.27	-0.61
Education	85 (48%)	71 (52%)	14 (33%)	27 (39%)	55 (53%)	5.06	-0.03	3.44	-0.06
Work	92 (50%)	76 (55%)	16 (34%)	36 (49%)	52 (49%)	5.98	-0.01	0.00	-0.99
Income	138 (75%)	107 (78%)	31 (67%)	53 (74%)	81 (76%)	1.89	-0.17	0.10	-0.75
Police/Judiciary	72 (42%)	59 (45%)	13 (34%)	23 (32%)	47 (49%)	1.33	-0.25	4.60	-0.03
Health Needs:									
Physical Health	86 (47%)	72 (52%)	14 (30%)	29 (39%)	55 (52%)	6.55	-0.01	3.03	-0.08
Mental Health	99 (53%)	73 (52%)	26 (57%)	43 (58%)	54 (51%)	0.27	-0.61	1.03	-0.31
Social Needs:									
Contact Family	59 (32%)	49 (35%)	10 (21%)	26 (34%)	32 (30%)	3.07	-0.08	0.33	-0.57
Contact Friends	25 (13%)	20 (14%)	5 (11%)	11 (15%)	14 (13%)	0.33	-0.57	0.09	-0.67
Leisure Activities	35 (19%)	30 (22%)	5 (11%)	16 (22%)	19 (18%)	2.82	-0.09	0.38	-0.54

Table 3: Responses to questions about good and bad qualities of social workers in the domain of basic needs

Housing
1. Do social workers help you?

Yes		150	(79%)		
a-1.	What is good about it?			a-2. What can be improved?	
	sw help to find a permanent place to live	74	(39%)	more houses available	48	(26%)
	sw help to find a temporary place to stay	56	(30%)	support should be given more quickly	47	(25%)
	sw help to arrange things	10	(5%)	more individual attention	12	(6%)
	sw stimulate and motivate	7	(4%)	better temporary residential centres	5	(3%)
	other	3	(2%)	nothing	28	(15%)
				other	8	(4%)
No		39	(21%)		
b-1.	Why not?			b-2. What can be improved?	
	sw do not help	26	(14%)	sw must show a greater effort	21	(11%)
	hy do the most work themselves	6	(3%)	more individual attention	5	(3%)
	other	7	(3%)	nothing	3	(2%)
				other	8	(5%)
		189	(100%)		185	(100%)

Education
1. Do social workers help you?

Yes		92	(47%)		
a-1.	What is good about it?			a-2. What can be improved?	
	sw help to find a school	48	(26%)	more support by the sw	19	(11%)
	sw stimulate and motivate	22	(12%)	more information about possibilities	10	(6%)
	sw help to register	9	(5%)	not too much pressure	10	(6%)
	sw help with schoolwork	9	(5%)	easier procedures to enter education	3	(2%)
	other	2	(1%)	nothing	34	(19%)
				other	11	(6%)
No		85	(53%)		
b-1.	Why not?			b-2. What can be improved?	
	no education is being followed	49	(27%)	more individual attention	16	(9%)
	it's not the sw's task to help in this domain	22	(12%)	more information	4	(2%)
	sw do not help	10	(5%)	nothing	52	(29%)
	hy does not want education	9	(5%)	other	18	(10%)
	other	4	(2%)		
		184	(100%)		177	(100%)

162

Table 3: Responses to questions about good and bad qualities of social workers in the domain of basic needs (cont)

Work

1. Do social workers help you?

Yes   85   (49%)

a-1.	What is good about it?			a-2. What can be improved?		
	sw help to find work	41	(22%)	more support by the sw	17	(9%)
	sw stimulate and motivate	34	(18%)	more jobs	10	(5%)
	sw find a job	10	(5%)	more motivation by the sw	7	(4%)
	other	6	(4%)	more independence for		
				the hy	2	(1%)
				nothing	29	(16%)
				other	25	(15%)

No   95   (51%)

b-1.	Why not?			b-2. What can be improved?		
	the responsibility of the hy	38	(20%)	sw should give better		
	hy doesn't work or want to			advice	9	(5%)
	work	17	(9%)	help should be quicker	7	(4%)
	hy is following an education	16	(9%)	not too much pressure	6	(3%)
	hy already had work	8	(4%)	first help in other domains	5	(3%)
	other	15	(9%)	nothing	45	(25%)
				other	16	(10%)
		185	(100%)		178	(100%)

Income

1. Do social workers help you?

Yes   139   (75%)

a-1.	What is good about it?			a-2. What can be improved?		
	sw make a financial plan	67	(37%)	budget is too low	29	(16%)
	sw help to apply for a benefit	38	(20%)	help should be quicker	21	(12%)
	sw help to solve financial			better arrangements for		
	debts	22	(12%)	debts	14	(8%)
	sw help to find an income	8	(4%)	more cooperation		
				between hy and sw	15	(8%)
	other	1	(2%)	more independence for		
				the hy	9	(5%)
				nothing	40	(22%)
				other	7	(5%)

No   46   (25%)

b-1.	Why not?			b-2. What can be improved?		
	hy arranged own income	13	(7%)	budget is too low	8	(4%)
	sw do not help	13	(7%)	sw should give more		
	hy has no problems with			support	11	(6%)
	money	9	(5%)	more independence for hy	3	(2%)
	other	12	(7%)	nothing	19	(10%)
				other	4	(2%)
		185	(100%)		180	(100%)

Table 3: Responses to questions about good and bad qualities of social workers in the domain of basic needs (cont)

Police/Judiciary
1. Do social workers help you?

Yes		72	(42%)			
a-1.	What is good about it?			a-2. What can be improved?		
	sw try to mediate	27	(15%)	sw should give higher		
	sw help to solve the problems			priority	12	(7%)
		20	(11%)	cooperation police/		
	sw contact police/judiciary	11	(6%)	judiciary/agencies	3	(2%)
	sw offer support and advice	10	(6%)	nothing	31	(19%)
	other	7	(4%)	Other	26	(17%)
No		99	(58%)			
b-1.	Why not?			b-2. What can be improved?		
	hy has no problems with			more support from sw	5	(3%)
	police/judiciary	57	(34%)			
	it's not the sw's task to help			more efficiency in the		
	in this domain	21	(12%)	support	4	(2%)
	problems were taken care of	10	(6%)	nothing	62	(38%)
	sw do not help in this domain	7	(4%)	other	19	(12%)
	other	4	(2%)			

Table 4: Responses to questions about good and bad qualities of social workers in the domain of health needs

Physical Health

1. Do social workers help you?

Yes 86 (46%)

a-1. What is good about it?

			a-2. What can be improved?		
sw check hy in with a doctor	34	(18%)	care should be better		
sw help to find a doctor	26	(14%)	organised	22	(11%)
			agencies need to have		
sw the agency has it's own			their own doctor	6	(3%)
doctor	20	(11%)	care should be provided		
			more quickly	4	(2%)
other	7	(4%)	nothing	40	(21%)
			other	13	(7%)

No 99 (54%)

b-1. Why not?

			b-2. What can be improved?		
hy help themselves	61	(33%)	care should be provided		
			more quickly	11	(6%)
there are no problems	17	(9%)	more attention for physical		
sw do not help in this domain	17	(9%)	problems	8	(4%)
other	6	(2%)	nothing	61	(37%)
			other	16	(9%)
	188	(100%)		181	(100%)

Mental Health

1. Do social workers help you?

Yes 99 (53%)

a-1. What is good about it?

			a-2. What can be improved?		
sw talk with hy	39	(21%)	more attention for		
sw refer to others for help	31	(17%)	problems	37	(17%)
sw listen, give support and			quick referral	8	(4%)
advice	23	(12%)	hy need some time to		
sw learn hy to deal with			calm down	6	(3%)
emotions	4	(2%)	nothing	29	(17%)
other	1	(1%)	other	17	(9%)

No 88 (47%)

b-1. Why not?

			b-2. What can be improved?		
hy do not want to discuss			more attention for		
their problems	29	(16%)	problems	23	(13%)
sw do not ask about problems	18	(10%)	sw should not interfere	8	(4%)
there are no problems	15	(8%)	hy need some time to		
sw can not help	14	(8%)	calm down	5	(3%)
hy help themselves	4	(2%)	sw should refer hy to		
			psychologist	4	(2%)
			nothing	32	(19%)
other	8	(3%)	other	9	(5%)
	186	(100%)		178	(100%)

Table 5: Responses to questions about good and bad qualities of social workers in the domain of social needs

Contact with Family

1. Do social workers help you?

Yes   59   (31%)

a-1.	What is good about it?			a-2. What can be improved?		
	sw establish contact with family	37	(20%)	more attention for problems	11	(6%)
	sw talk with family	12	(6%)	sw should not interfere	10	(5%)
	sw try to find family	3	(2%)	sw should establish first contact	6	(3%)
	other	8	(4%)	nothing	22	(12%)
				other	11	(6%)

No   130   (68%)

b-1.	Why not?			b-2. What can be improved?		
	sw should not interfere	44	(23%)	sw should not interfere	30	(16%)
	hy does not want help	20	(11%)	sw should give more attention to family	10	(6%)
	hy does not want contact	18	(10%)	sw should work more quickly	6	(3%)
	contact with parents is good	17	(9%)	nothing	64	(36%)
	hy arrange contact themselves	9	(5%)	other	12	(7%)
	sw can not solve the problems	7	(4%)			
	other	12	(6%)			
		187	(100%)		182	(100%)

Contact with Friends

Yes   25   (13%)

a-1.	What is good about it?			a-2. What can be improved?		
	sw help to find a friend	12	(6%)	possibility to bring friends along	5	(3%)
	sw talk about friendship	10	(5%)	hy must help themselves	5	(3%)
	nothing	1	(1%)	sw should give more support	3	(2%)
	other	4	(2%)	nothing	11	(6%)
				other	3	(2%)

No   163   (87%)

b-1.	Why not?			b-2. What can be improved?		
	it is not the task of sw	56	(30%)	sw should not interfere	46	(25%)
	hy does not need help	45	(23%)	more possibilities for contact	8	(4%)
	hy wants to select own friends	23	(12%)	better rules for meeting peers	4	(2%)
	sw can not help	20	(11%)	nothing	86	(46%)
	hy already has friends	9	(5%)	other	14	(7%)
	other	11	(5%)			
		191	(100%)		185	(100%)

Table 5: Responses to questions about good and bad qualities of social workers in the domain of social needs (Cont)

No		163	(87%)			
b-1.	Why not?			b-2. What can be improved?		
	it is not the task of sw	56	(30%)	sw should not interfere	46	(25%)
	hy does not need help	45	(23%)	more possibilities for		
	hy wants to select own			contact	8	(4%)
	friends	23	(12%)	better rules for meeting		
	sw can not help	20	(11%)	peers	4	(2%)
	hy already has friends	9	(5%)	nothing	86	(46%)
	other	11	(5%)	other	14	(7%)
		191	(100%)		185	(100%)

Leisure Activities

Yes		35	(19%)			
a-1.	What is good about it?			a-2. What can be improved?		
	sw help to find activities	13	(7%)	more activities for hy	15	(8%)
	sw help to make a plan for			nothing	11	(6%)
	the day	8	(4%)			
	sw organise activities	7	(4%)	other	10	(6%)
	sw give financial support	6	(3%)			
	other	5	(3%)			
No		151	(81%)			
b-1.	Why not?			b-2. What can be improved?		
	it is not the task of sw	79	(44%)	sw should not interfere	33	(19%)
	hy does not need help	52	(28%)	more activities for hy	19	(11%)
	problems are not discussed	10	(5%)	sw should be involved		
	other	4	(2%)	more	10	(6%)
				nothing	61	(36%)
				other	14	(8%)
		184	(100%)		173	(100%)

Index